# Consciously Create Your Dream Life with the Law Of Attraction:

*25 Practical Techniques & Meditations to Supercharge Your Manifestations, Raise Your Vibration, & Start Manifesting*

Spirituality and Soulfulness

# Contents

# SPECIAL BONUS!

**GET 333 AFFIRMATIONS SENT DIRECTLY TO YOU + ACCESS TO ALL OF OUR FUTURE PUBLISHED BOOKS!**

**SIGN UP BELOW TO CLAIM YOUR BONUS!**

*SCAN W/ YOUR CAMERA TO JOIN!*

# Introduction

What do you dream of manifesting in your life? Is it more money, a new home, a baby, lasting romance, recognition, or a job promotion?

Part of human nature is the strong urge to experience a grander, more liberating life, and that's a good thing. For ancient civilizations, desire was a conflicting topic. They didn't know whether to condemn or celebrate it.

Some believed it was good and divine to embrace the urges deep within us. Others thought it would lead to evil and suffering. That, in turn, created a lot of unhealthy beliefs that have stuck around. And that's partly why we experience so much frustration.

In every generation, there have always been the few individuals who go against the grain. These people find a way to escape the belief of desire as evil and realize that following our heart's desires is not only our birthright, but also a natural and effortless process that summons divine providence.

I'm sure you've come across someone's story on social media where they shared how they went from rags to riches without any unique talent. The hard-working and talented Will Smith is not only an inspiration for our generation, but he's also a great teacher demonstrating how anyone can create their dream lifestyle. In an interview, Will Smith said, "You just need to decide what it's gonna be, who you're gonna be, you just decide. And then, from that point, the universe is going to get out of your way. It's water. It wants to move and go around stuff." In other words, when we become absolutely committed to a particular path, and we follow through on that decision, the universe is always there to support us. The key here is to move in the same direction as the "water" of life, not against it.

If you've ever come across the outlandish Wesley "Million Dollar" Virgin, you've heard him praise the law of attraction and how it helped him manifest millions of dollars, deals with the Kardashians, and the exuberant lifestyle he often portrays on social media. But even if you're not a fan of guys driving fancy cars and living large, you might have heard people talk about how they manifested their dream job.

Megan shared a post on Facebook describing how badly she'd wanted to get a new job and move back home. The problem was she was in the entertainment industry and working on the West Coast. It felt impossible at first. A friend introduced her to the same teachings you're about to learn in this book, and within two years of practicing, Megan was back on the East Coast, living near her mom and working at her dream job. She credits this life-altering experience to the remarkable law of attraction. The stories are endless, and I could tell you about the woman who healed herself of breast cancer, the man who finally found the love of his life, and the couple who struggled for years to get pregnant until they discovered the power of this law. But if all I did were share stories, this book would end up being a series of case studies, which it is not. So, rather than talk about how others have succeeded, let's focus on how you can finally manifest your dream life through the law of attraction.

## A Novice or a Veteran of LOA?

Most people invest in a book of this nature for two reasons. Either you're new to the topic of "manifesting" or you've been trying to make it work for a long time, and nothing is happening. Regardless of your reason, you came to the right place because this is where we answer some of the most pressing questions law of attraction students have. Questions such as:

- Is the law of attraction genuine or just some new-age scam?
- Can I really have the thing I've always dreamed of?
- Are money, success, love, happiness, health, and great relationships all within my grasp? If so, why am I still waiting for everything to happen, and how can I finally make it happen?

# What This Book Can Do for You

This book will give you a new level of clarity when it comes to understanding the law of attraction, how it really works, and how to finally become more in control of your manifestations. Much of what's published online regarding this universal law is only half the equation. This book will give you the complete equation and walk you through the simple yet profound steps that will finally make you a master manifester. Everything you've ever needed to create the change you desire in life is laid out in simple, easy-to-follow chapters, so you'll never have to wait in confusion and doubt again. The best part is that your dreams will take form in the most natural way possible (it's almost going to feel silly that you ever doubted your ability to create a life you love). Suppose you've dabbled in personal development and the law of attraction for a while; you might be experiencing lots of frustration and despair because none of the tricks and techniques you've been taught have yielded anything worthwhile. Understand, however, that whatever books you've read, gurus you've followed, or seminars you've attended haven't been wrong. In fact, many of the gurus I've come across are brilliant. But it might be that a vital piece of the puzzle was missing from the information you received, which made it impossible for you to complete your success puzzle. Whether your previous knowledge was incomplete or you misunderstood the proper way of implementing the teaching doesn't make a difference. What matters is that you're here now, and you don't need to worry about what went wrong last time because in your hands, you hold a complete and comprehensive law of attraction guide that caters to both first-time manifesters and veterans.

Most readers don't land on this book until they've gone through countless others. But if you're one of the lucky few who is just getting started, congratulations on finding the perfect kick-off point! You'll get a solid foundation for working with the law as well as all the necessary pieces of your success puzzle so that things can finally fall into place for you.

Your life is a masterpiece designed to perfection. Did you know that? It's time to understand how to put things in their proper order so you can experience the joys of being a grand masterpiece.

# Why the Law of Attraction Hasn't Been "Working" for You

Let's set the record straight right off the bat. One of the common themes I hear when LOA students complain about their unmanifested dreams is the fact that "it isn't working for them." If you've been studying and attempting to apply this law into your life, and it failed to give you the desired outcome, that's not to say that the law isn't working.

Although we'll cover the long-form version of this widespread error and help you shift into the right approach within the following few chapters, the short version you should grasp now is the following: the law of attraction isn't some modern technique or an invention by the people who wrote *The Secret*; it is a universal law that is immutable, incorruptible, and ever-present. It was in operation long before you became aware of it and it will continue working long after you're gone. So, approaching this law like some-thing that may or may not be working already puts you on the negative side of things, and that's what we must change. There's an entire chapter to help you iron out the misunderstandings and myths surrounding the law of attraction so you can finally stop experiencing disillusionment with the lack of results that might be prevalent in your current reality.

LOA isn't a load of crap. It works—but only if you put in the work. If you learn about this law and take little action, it may appear that it doesn't work for you. You might even be tempted to buy "a better book" or another program, but that won't solve anything. The real issue is that you need to develop a fundamental understanding of where the law of attraction comes from and how your mind works. Failure to do this increases the likelihood that you'll approach it from the wrong premise, resulting in undesirable outcomes.

## The Key to Getting Your Dream Life

Before you can experience just how good and powerful the universal laws are, you will need to make one critical commitment to yourself—that you'll do everything in your power to rid yourself of doubt daily. Have you realized that doubts and fears have crippled your life? That these are the real enemies you're having to contend with when it comes to manifesting your dream life? If not, then permit me to give you a wake-up call. Social conditioning has caused us to live exclusively in physical reality. What we cannot see, hear, taste, smell, or touch is considered "unreal." That's a problem, you know?

The visible part of life—what we call "real"—is but a tiny insignificant fraction in the grand stage of life. For thousands of years, sages have tried to help us come to this realization, but the masses continue to doubt, which perpetuates the human struggle. Science has now caught up with what religion and spirituality taught long ago. Scientists confirm that everything our physical senses consider real in our universe only makes up 4% of what's actually there —the stars, planets, and galaxies (including ourselves and the nature surrounding us). So, what's the other 96%? Stuff that even the best astronomers and our best technology can neither detect, see, or comprehend at the moment. They've opted to name this invisible and dominant stuff dark energy and dark matter. So what does that mean for us?

We live in a world that exists in a universe made up of who-knows-what. The part that we can easily comprehend—i.e., the visible stuff—is truly the minority, implying that we can never fully understand the game of life and the universal laws if we stubbornly choose to live based on physical sensations.

A reality test:

Imagine for a moment that you were preparing dinner and accidentally touched a hot pan with your bare hands. Do you have any doubt about the burn and accompanying pain you'd experience?

Now I'd like you to bring to mind just one thing you've always desired to have. As you think about having that thing or experience, does it feel as real as the first exercise of getting your fingers burned? Does this desirable thing cause you to feel more doubt just because at the moment, you lack the visceral and physical sensations of its reality?

If you're like most people, getting burned by a hot stove is undoubtedly real. Manifesting love or that dream home is less "real," and therefore, the brain refuses to process that data and keeps you in the current reality. This, right here, is the key to becoming a masterful manifestor. You must reprogram your mind and brain to work with the invisible laws so your inner vision and inner world can be just as dominant as the visible outer world you're accustomed to. Just as scientists realize that the actual game is understanding more of the invisible universe, you must become your own scientist and embark on an adventure that enables you to focus more on your invisible nature. The manifested, visible aspect of your life is but a tiny speck of the hidden inner side. When you can eliminate all doubt in the process of pursuing a dream, you will, in effect, materialize anything you set your mind on. It's so simple and so profound, yet few get it.

And just like that, I've laid out the crown jewel that you've been looking for. If you stopped reading this book at this point and worked on unlocking that invisible power that you possess, you'd reap the rewards of the law of attraction. Assuming, however, that you'd like a guide to help you on this new adventure, keep turning the pages of this book. The following chapters are designed to take out all the guesswork so you can finally have both the knowledge and the faith to pursue any dream that makes you come alive. Let's go.

# Chapter 1

## The Universal Laws of Success Defined

*"The basic laws of the universe are simple, but because our senses are limited, we can't grasp them. There is a pattern in creation."*

— Albert Einstein

It's still too early in the world of modern science to get collective agreement that universal laws of success are a real thing, but we are slowly closing that gap with every discovery. Albert Einstein said that everything in the world is energy. He was right, and that gave us a solid starting point when it came to understanding ourselves and the people, animals, and immaterial things surrounding us.

A good place to begin our quest for masterful manifestation is realizing that everything (and I mean everything) is energy. Not only that, but this energy is also in constant motion. The gadget you're using to read this book; the chair, bed, table in your home; your favorite coffee mug, a tree, a plane, a flower— they are all in constant motion. And so are you. The accepted name for this motion is vibration, and since everything vibrates, it does so at a specific frequency that is in harmony with its own nature.

***Pro tip:***

"Order is heaven's first law." That means that the universe always operates harmoniously, so if you want to change from a specific frequency to another, you'll need to get yourself into harmony with the working of the law for it to work. It will serve you well to remember and repeat this statement several times each day.

# What They Don't Tell You about the Law of Attraction

Now that you understand that everything is energy and that vibration at a specific frequency determines what that thing is, it should be evident that the law of attraction is actually not the primary law. If you've already come to this conclusion, you're right. One needs to learn other fundamental laws before subsidiary laws like LOA make complete sense. Remember when I said doubt is your worst enemy? The only way to cure doubt is to soak yourself in true knowledge—the kind that enables you to know with certainty that what you're dealing with is a reliable ally, not a gimmick. To do this, we need to discuss the major universal principles that explain how energy, frequencies, and vibrations work. This book will go over the seven main principles that put you directly in harmony with the law of attraction. By the end of this chapter, I want it to be clear to you that the law of attraction is a subtle, subsidiary, universal law that is ever at work.

Why do LOA gurus make it seem like LOA only works if you have a vision board, think positive thoughts, and practice affirmations three times a day? Probably for the same reasons a doctor prescribes flu medicines to sick patients. He knows all they need is to sleep enough, hydrate, increase vitamin C intake, and stop stressing until the natural cycle of the virus runs its course. However, telling that to a sick person who believes only in medication will not do that person any good. So, the good doctor will give you pills to knock you out so that nature can do its thing and heal you. The medicines aren't bad, and in many cases, they are necessary.

Similarly, LOA techniques aren't bad, and in many cases, they are indispensable. But don't get things twisted. You're not only invoking the law when you do these things; the law of attraction works at every moment of your waking and sleeping life. It follows precise lines of operations and only serves as the manager who ensures things of a like nature are interacting. But if LOA is the servant manager, who is the boss determining what it should do?

Enter the natural laws of success.

## Laws of Success

Although we're choosing to title these laws the laws of success, they might as well be known as the laws of nature or the laws of life because they apply to everything in material existence. The Oxford English Dictionary defines "natural law" as "an observable law relating to natural phenomena."

When you incorporate the knowledge of these laws into your consciousness, you will have the ability to effortlessly create the life of your dreams, and success shall be yours. But before you can master manifesting, you need a better grasp of the concept of law, for it is the process by which the unmanifest becomes the manifest. Everything you recognize in this material world has come about through the law. The law operates in three distinct domains: Spirit, mind, and body. Just as we know electricity moves from a higher potential to a lower potential, so does creation: it takes place in the higher realm first and then moves to the lower realm, with Spirit being the higher realm and the body (physical) being the lowest realm. So when we talk about manifesting, it's a process that must initiate from the highest domain; it then culminates in materialization at the physical level. The laws of the universe make this entire process possible, and when we understand them and apply them to our lives, anything we want can be attracted and created. These laws govern everything that happens, and they are neither good nor bad; they are neutral and exact in their operation.

Now, let's overview each of the primary natural laws before discussing the LOA in great detail.

## The Law of Divine Oneness

This law dictates that Unity is the underlying order in the universe. At the highest level, that of Source or Spirit, there is only oneness, for if there were to be two equal powers not of a like nature, we wouldn't be dealing with the All-Originating Life Principle.

So now we see that everything is connected to everything else. That means we are always connected to the All-Originating Life Principle/God/Source Energy. This Source is everywhere at once and permeates through all things, both manifest and unmanifest. You and the rock that stubbed your toe, the stars in the galaxy, your neighbor's dog, and anything or anyone else you can think of are made of the same stuff and share the same Source origin. It also means that everything you could ever desire is already connected to you because it can only come from that same Source. You are inseparable from every good thing you wish to have, but you lack the awareness to perceive that connection. As you study this material and increase your awareness of this law of oneness and the awareness of God, you'll start to experience this shift.

Remember Einstein's discovery that everything is energy? He was right. Everything consists of, and exists, as energy. Your subatomic particles aren't fixed; in fact, there's a ceaseless motion happening right this moment, and there's a natural flow into and out of you even as you read the words on this page. An exchange is taking place between you and everything in your environment. When you think about your worst enemy, an exchange is happening; if you think about that desire that burns in your heart, an exchange is happening as well, and it determines whether you move closer to full materialization or further away.

One of the main reasons we need to start with this underlying premise before discussing the law of attraction is that without this fundamental understanding, the law of attraction or the other laws discussed in this chapter won't make much sense. However, if you realize that the game of life originates from one Source and that materialization is merely one end (the lower end) of an incredible life equation, then you'll at once see how all these laws work together to serve a single purpose—the expansion and progression of life.

## The Law of Vibration

The law of vibration states that anything and every-thing in the universe (visible or invisible to the naked eye) can be broken down into its purest and most basic form: pure energy. And this pure energy resonates and exists as a vibratory frequency. Think about all the material stuff in your environment. Now, think about your feelings, body, and thoughts. All of these possess a distinct vibrational frequency. Do you know what the difference is between sand on the beach and the glass sitting in your kitchen cabi-net? Vibrational frequency. The rate at which they vibrate determines whether they remain sand or transform into glass. Isn't that cool?

Well, if you think that's cool, then consider how your thoughts, feelings, and actions determine what vibra-tional frequency you experience. Similar to the vibrational pattern of the sand turning into glass, your vibrational frequency and what you choose as the dominant state determines what your life trans-forms into. By consciously choosing the rate at which your thoughts, feelings, and actions vibrate, you're deciding which conditions, people, and things will resonate with you and, in turn, what shows up in your reality. In other words, your thoughts are insep-arably connected to the rest of the universe.

Unlike sand, you have the power to choose a particular frequency and thereby the autonomy to determine what you'll become. This is where things get good. As you deliberately choose the frequency, a secondary law we call the law of attraction is automatically set into motion to match you with anything and everything that possesses identical frequency. How you monitor and control that vibrational frequency is a lesson we'll get into later in the book.

For now, we need to recognize that the law of vibration is the fundamental principle backing the law of attraction. If you don't understand and learn to control your vibration, you'll always struggle to understand and align with the positive aspect of the law of attraction. Mainstream media is so obsessed with LOA that they've forgotten to educate personal development students on this fundamental principle. That's why so many people assume LOA is a scam or an artificial idea.

The key concept about this law:

> *Everything vibrates, and the only difference between one object and another is the vibration rate. For example, something static like a*

*desk vibrates more slowly than something
dynamic and alive such as your body.*

Like everything else in the universe, your thoughts
vibrate at different frequencies depending on the
nature of the thought. Through our power of choice,
we can direct and determine the frequency of
thought and, in turn, the emotional state of our body,
which invariably determines what we experience in
life thanks to the ever-faithful law of attraction.

## The Law of Polarity

Is it possible to have an inside without an outside?
Up without down? Light without dark or hot
without cold? Have you ever asked yourself if you'd
know happiness if sadness didn't exist as the polar
opposite? Polarity, or the law of opposites, is a
natural law in life, and it enables manifestation.
Spirit is the polar opposite of matter, and although
Spirit exists independent of matter, the two are
necessary to form a complete whole. The material
world exists at the level of duality, and contrary to
mass thinking, the two can harmoniously co-exist
because each serves a divine purpose. Everything in
our world has its pair of opposites, and these opposites are identical in nature but different in degree.

To understand this principle of polarity, you'll need to devote more time learning how to maintain balance, focus, and detachment from the distractions of the material world. And although polarity is a natural law, it is by no means an absolute. In other words, there is a law greater and higher than the law of polarity (the Great Law or Divine Oneness) that is at the origin of all these laws. But to understand the creative process and manifestation, we can see the necessity of the law of polarity because it's the only way for Unity to enjoy multiplicity and diversity in its own creativeness. So, think about this for a moment. Can you accurately and precisely point where night stops and day begins? Or where cold stops and heat begins? A little consideration and practical observation will show that this isn't possible. That's because they are all two sides of the same coin. That's what the famous author of *Think and Grow Rich*, Napoleon Hill, said: "Every adversity, every failure, and every heartache carries with it the seed of an equivalent or greater benefit."

The fundamental concept of this law:

> *This law of polarity states that everything has a polar opposite, and not only that, but it's*

*also equal and opposite. That means that if it were six feet from the bottom of something to the top, it would be six feet from the top to the bottom of the same thing; it cannot be any other way. So how does this apply to you? With this newfound knowledge, you can use this law of polarity in your favor. Instead of getting stuck on one perspective, you can see both sides of a situation, circumstance, or person. This law can help you feel empowered and inspired even in the middle of challenges by helping you activate and consciously use your mental faculties.*

## The Law of Perpetual Transmutation

In his famous little book *The Science of Getting Rich*, author Wallace D. Wattles talks about the law of perpetual transmutation. He teaches that energy from the formless realm is constantly flowing into the material world and taking form. Remember what we said about electricity moving from a higher potential to a lower potential? Your formed reality moves along the same lines in that the limitless, inexhaustible ENERGY flows downward and takes form along the lines you've established in your life. It happens in your life, and to every other formed thing in the universe. As old forms reach their climax, they give way for new forms to emerge from the invisible, hidden energy of the universe. Suffice it to say that there is a constant moving into and out of form that's ever taking place across our universe. Motion or movement is something we cannot control or stop. Life is ever moving forward and upward, seeking a better, higher, and grander expression of itself. With the proper awareness and illuminated mental faculties, you can learn to harness this inexhaustible, ever-present energy and direct it to take whatever form you desire. The energy flows into your consciousness all the time, but you're not deliberately guiding it, and that's the main problem to solve.

The key concept of this law:

> *The law of perpetual transmutation reinforces that everything we can see, hear, smell, taste, or touch—and our emotions—are all manifestations of energy. And that this energy is ever in constant motion, taking form and going out of form. Change is, therefore, the only thing that is constant in life. Since we know that energy can neither be created nor*

*destroyed, we can rest in the total assurance that we will always have this primordial substance to form whatever our minds can conceive. The real challenge is accurately harnessing, guiding, directing, and shaping this formless into a form that we desire. How do we do this? That's what this book intends to help you discover and master. Here's a good hint: it has everything to do with how you're operating your mind.*

## The Law of Rhythm

Have you ever noticed that everything in nature moves to a specific rhythm? Watch the birds flying, the bees moving from flower to flower, or even the rain falling. The law of rhythm is a natural law of life, dictating that everything vibrates and moves in specific rhythmic patterns. These rhythms establish seasons, cycles, stages of development, and other patterns. You can observe it in the rising and setting of the sun and moon, the ebb and flow of tides, the coming and going of the seasons, and the rhythmic swing of consciousness and unconsciousness.

In *The Kybalion*, it is written that "Everything flows, out and in; everything has its tides; all things rise and fall; the pendulum swing manifests in everything; the measure of the swing to the right is the measure of the swing to the left; rhythm compensates." That's quite poetic, and it also gives us a deeper look into how the laws all work together. Although we describe them as individual laws, I hope you can see how they seem to blend into the One GREAT Law Of Life.

Whenever the tide goes out, you can be sure it must come back in. We can observe this law in almost everything we care about, i.e., health, weather patterns, relationships, and even the economy. And although it's easier to believe that there's an orderly pattern to this law when talking about the seasons of the year, that same order is ever-present in our lives. Let's say you've realized that you're at the peak of your career or fitness level. At some point, you'll experience a drop that might be drastic or moderate. There's nothing wrong with this shift; it's simply a sign that you're due for some new changes. A rest period is always advised, after which you should focus on growing to a better and higher level of potential.

The key concept of this law:

*There's an ever-present and orderly, rhythmic pattern to everything in existence. This swinging is constant, and depending on where we are on that swing, we experience feelings, events, and conditions that match that particular state. So, it's okay if you realize that you're not always happy, energetic, or mentally sharp; no one is. We all experience swings from one end of life's pendulum to the other. If you're on a downswing, know that the swing will change, and things will get better. It will help if you focus your mind on the feelings you prefer instead of wallowing in the reality of what you don't have. Masters of LOA realize the power of this law and invest a lot of energy mastering their emotions to maintain balance. That way, the swing doesn't go too extreme on either end of the emotional scale, making it easier to experience less dramatic swings.*

## The Law of Relativity

This law is of great benefit because its main gift is teaching us the power of perspective. I might have woken up a bit tired today because I worked late last night, and that might seem like a good enough reason to go into work feeling grumpy and ungrateful. But the only result of possessing such an attitude is expanding negativity. Think about it for a moment— days when you leave the house in a hostile, angry state tend to be the days when more negativity finds you. Someone bumps your car, the traffic is a night-mare, a colleague spills coffee on your white shirt, or your boss yells at you. Now, imagine if, before leaving the house, you give yourself a pep talk and consider how many unemployed, homeless, and poverty-stricken people are wishing they could have what you have. You don't even need to look very far because I'm sure even in your community, there are many struggling to make ends meet. Yet, here you are with a job and a roof over your head, good food, a car, and the ability to invest in educational material like this that can change your life forever. Is your life really that bad?

From a metaphysical and spiritual point of view, this is what the law of relativity is here to teach us. Our seeming bad is only relatively bad. How we make that comparison determines our perspective, atti-tude, and results in life. If you want to feel good about your life, stop comparing it to curated Instagram accounts of people who spend hours doing photoshoots while you spend most of your day behind a desk, earning your income. No matter how bad you perceive your situation to be, there's someone out there who is in a worse position. It's all relative.

The key concept of this law:

> *Everything in our physical world is only made real by its relationship or comparison to something else. In studying this law, we realize that all laws are related and correspond with one another.*

Light exists because we compare it to dark. We call something good because we've compared it to something we consider bad. Therefore, nothing is all good or all bad, negative or positive, but our perception determines a thing to be what we say it is. The meaning we give something in life relative to ourselves makes that thing what it is relative to us. So, you can choose to see the problems in your life as bad (things that are out to destroy you), or you can see them as lessons that enable you to uncover and discover what you're really made of. In other words, you can make this law work for you or against you. It's all just a matter of perspective, and regardless of which stand you take, you will be right.

## The Law of Cause and Effect

This is one of my favorite laws to study, and I think I understand why Ralph Waldo Emerson called this "the Law of Laws." The premise of this law is that action and reaction are equal and opposite. Whatever you transmit (you're continuously transmitting a signal) always comes back in equal measure, whether you recognize it or not. It may not come back in a shape or form that makes sense to you, but vibrationally speaking, the essence of the form will match the signals you sent out to the universe. Your signal initiates cause, and the universe responds with a perfectly matching effect. It's a beautiful thing when you think about it, but, yes, it can also be an awful thing if we're constantly transmitting unpleasant signals. That's why we have an entire chapter discussing the various ways you can start sending the right signals to the universe.

Your physical health, money, and relationships are all effects. That's why, in the Bible, you will find a teaching of Christ saying that we must seek first the kingdom of God, and all the rest will follow. The great secret here is that "the rest" are the material manifestations you desire. These effects come only when you (the cause) have focused on sending out the right signals instead of forcing the effects to happen.

The key concept of this law:

> *Every human thought, word, and deed is a*
> *cause that sets off a wave of energy*
> *throughout the universe. In turn, the universe*
> *responds with an equal and opposite reaction,*
> *creating the desirable or undesirable effect.*

# Chapter 2

## *The Universal Law of Attraction*

*"Once you make a decision, the universe conspires to make it happen."*

— Ralph Waldo Emerson

With the fundamental laws now in view, it's time to discuss the main law covered by this book: the law of attraction. We mentioned in the previous chapter that one could not fully understand or advantageously use this law without a proper grasp of the law of vibration. That's because vibration and attraction go hand in hand. The law of vibration is the primary law, and through vibrational harmony, attraction (the second law) is set into motion in precise ways.

## What Is the Law of Attraction?

Simply put, that which is like, unto itself is drawn. In other words, things of like nature and vibrational frequencies tend to gravitate toward each other. Nothing is attracted randomly; everything works according to natural law.

In our case, thoughts vibrate at a specific frequency, and the feelings, words, and actions we take determine what the law of attraction will match us with. If your dominant energy transmission is negative, you will attract negative energies. Likewise, if you predominantly transmit positive energy, you will attract positive energies. The law of attraction doesn't initiate selection; its job is to facilitate the completion of the manifesting process.

At this very moment, you're being guided and influenced by universal forces you aren't even aware of. Just like the law of gravity, these laws are always working, either for or against you. The fact that you're reading this book isn't a random act. Your transmission to the universe made it possible for this match to occur, and if with every chapter you're feeling more and more resonance, it means you've raised your vibrational frequency to match the words, meaning, and the power of these laws. The good news is that learning to work with the law of attraction and the other laws isn't rocket science, and the more you immerse yourself in this book and proactively work on raising that vibrational state, the better your life becomes. It's not at a future time; it's happening now, at this moment. You might be thinking right now, "Wait a minute...the law of attraction is working now, already? Is that true? Is the law actually real?"

## Is there any truth to the law of attraction?

The uninitiated and the pessimists often scoff at the idea of universal laws that bring prosperity. They view the law of attraction as "woo woo" stuff, but the truth is, great philosophers, spiritual teachers, and wisdom seekers have been talking about this and all the laws mentioned earlier for thousands of years. And when you understand how the law of attraction works, you too can use it to change your life for the better and create a fantastic future.

# Origins of the Law of Attraction

If we look back far enough, we can find the roots of this law in various ancient practices and Eastern teachings. Don't get me wrong—no one called it the law of attraction back then. But that doesn't mean people weren't aware of it and working with it in their daily lives.

## Did Buddha and Jesus Christ know about the law of attraction?

In both Buddhist and Christian teachings, we find statements and lessons that enable us to understand the importance of aligning with this law. For instance, the Buddha famously said that our thoughts make us what we are. "We are what we think. All that we are arises with our thoughts. With our thoughts, we make the world." - Buddha.

In Matthew 7:7-8, we are told, "Ask, and it will be given you; seek and you will find; knock and the door will be opened to you. For everyone who asks receives; the one who seeks finds; and to the one who knocks, the door will be opened."

While I am not here to debate whether these religious teachings directly refer to the law of attraction as it is taught in mainstream media (I know many Christians who may disagree with that notion), I intend to show you that the underlying principle is valid. You don't need to be religious or spiritual to recognize and realize the power of the law of attraction. Still, many find that this quest often leads to spiritual awakening because we deal with forces larger than our ordinary human awareness.

In modern times—more specifically, as recent as the 19th century—the term "law of attraction" has become a genuine concept. While several authors played a vital role in this development, two specific ones stand out: Helena Blavatsky, who gave spiritual instruction and guidance in various countries and wrote the book called *The Secret Doctrine*; and Thomas Troward, who is often described as a mystic Christian and wrote several essays on thought power and mental science. These individuals believed that life was meant to be an "inside out" game. These trailblazers inspired a new generation of thinkers and writers in the 20th century, including, but not limited to, William Walker Atkinson, who wrote over 100 books. A famous statement Atkinson made is that we generally find what we seek. Another great practitioner and teacher of that century was Wallace Delois Wattles, who wrote the famous book *The Science of Getting Rich* (published in 1910). He inspired several teachers, some of whom are alive right now, as we shall see later on.

Yet, perhaps no man has had a more significant impact on self-development and the understanding of these laws than Napoleon Hill, a journalist who spent decades studying Andrew Carnegie, Henry Ford, and some of the richest men of his time. The outcome was his book *Think and Grow Rich*, which continues to be a sensation today. By the mid-to-late 20th century, a new kind of law of attraction movement began when Jerry and Esther Hicks rose to prominence in the 1980s, purporting to channel messages from non-physical beings known collectively as "Abraham." They made the law of attraction mainstream talk, written several books, and conducted seminars where thousands of people have gathered to talk about it. With that came a boom in various teachers, some more known than others (Dr. Wayne Dyer, Louise Hay, and many more), aiming to spread the knowledge of manifesting a good life through the law of attraction. In more recent history, dating back to just a few years ago when Rhonda Byrne's book and film *The Secret* came out, the law of attraction went from a niche interest to a global sensation with lots of publicity. The speakers on that film included Jack Canfield, Bob Proctor, Joe Vitale, Marie Diamond, and Michael Beckwith, all of whom became overnight celebrities. Now we also have stars like Oprah, Will Smith, and Conor McGregor, who all credit the law of attraction for the success they've attained.

While there's still a lot of debate over the law of attraction, one thing is certain. Interest in this law isn't going to die anytime soon for the people who have chosen to take a more proactive role in their lives. I have spent years researching everything to do with this law, and over time, I've learned to ground myself in universal principles (not man-made ideas) when working with this law. Discovering LOA changed my life, and it's my intention you experience the same. It all begins with the understanding that you have more power than you think, and as Buddha said, you are what you think all day long.

So, what are you thinking all day long?

# Thoughts Have Magnetic Power

Would you believe me if I told you that your thoughts are why your life is as it is?

Whether you're miserable and living in the worst of conditions or ecstatic about your life, the underlying factor is the quality of your dominant thoughts. If you're still on the fence about this idea, stick with me and suspend your disbelief at least until this book is over. Then, you can decide what's true.

Have you ever stopped to think about where ideas come from? Where do thoughts originate, and where do they go once you're done obsessing about something? The common trap is to worry and obsess over our fears without ever considering the cost of such habits.

Imagine you hear a rumor at work that there would be layoffs in your department. You spend the subsequent months worrying, getting anxious, and thinking about all the worst-case scenarios that might happen if you got that letter. Fortunately, you don't get that termination letter, but you do get a pay cut. On the other hand, your colleague Sally ended up with a promotion and became head of the department at your company.

What just happened here? You both faced the same experience at work, but somehow, she came out better than you and everyone who got laid off. There are, of course, several logical reasons you could state to justify why Sally had such a different outcome, and you'd be right.

But at a fundamental level, this little example illustrates the power of thoughts in our lives and how we are each recreating reality to match our dominant thinking.

You might have heard statements like, "You become what you think," "Your thoughts create your reality," "Your thoughts are magnetic, and they create your experiences," "You become what you believe," "Every thought we think is creating our future," and so on. And you might have thought, "That's a cute way of looking at life."

Well, I'm here to offer a life-altering lesson: every experience you've had, both good and bad, had its seed in your thinking. And every future experience is seeded in the thought patterns you're entertaining. It's a simple concept, but not easy to accept.

## Are you paying attention to what you're thinking?

Most of us don't do a good job directing our thought energy. We claim we want more money, but spend most of our time thinking and talking about poverty and lack of financial abundance. Those seeking love claim they desire it, but more often than not, you'll catch them remarking, "All the good ones are taken," or "My partner always cheats on me." Here's another eye-opener: if you plan for success and prepare for failure, you will always get what you prepared for.

Read that last statement until it's embedded in your mind because if you can just make that one shift, you'll see things change almost instantly.

When we say thoughts have power, we mean it. Everything in the universe is energy, as Einstein already established. Your thoughts vibrate energetically at a specific frequency, and the laws of success, including the law of attraction, always respond to your most dominant thought frequency.

So, even if you attend a law of attraction seminar and fill yourself up with affirmations, claiming bold desires for yourself over that three-day event, then you go home and spend the rest of the week intensely worried, doubting, and entertaining fearful thoughts, guess what the outcome will be?

## Does Our Brain Play a Role in This Too?

Your brain consists of a tight network of nerve cells, all interacting with one another and generating a massive electrical field. This description isn't something I just made up—ask any scientist or doctor, and they'll tell you we have standard medical equipment that can detect your electric field. Your entire body is an electric field, but it's concentrated chiefly around your head because that's where the bulk of your nerve cells are. Next time you feel the shock of static electricity, remind yourself that it's not magic; it's scientific proof that your body is an energy field.

The cool thing is that this means that the wave patterns that make up your brain waves are governed by the same equations governing the electromagnetic spectrum, light particles, and everything else in the universe. So, basically, the light seen coming from a star and the energy readings from your brain are the same type. Your thoughts, being energy, are formed within this electric field. The measurable perturbations and disturbances in the brain's overall electric field are your actual thoughts in action. That means that right this instant, as you're reading this book, the thoughts you're thinking and the words your mind are processing appear as electrical impulses that can be measured in your brain if you had a few wires hooked up between your head and a machine.

Hence, thoughts really are energy! And since we are conscious beings operating this force field, we can choose how to manipulate this electric field. We can also decide which part of the randomness around us we're affected by and, in turn, how to influence *it* as well because we cannot separate ourselves from the environment. This property of entanglement, already established in quantum mechanics, enables us to effect change in our environment. Our brains are transceivers, able to receive and send signals into the "quantum soup" through the highly coherent frequencies of thoughts.

The higher the frequency of our thought/brainwave, the higher our consciousness, which also means the more powerful we become in manifesting the desired outcome. In a practical sense that's easy to "feel" your way into, think of it this way:

Thought energy moves at certain speeds. Lower thought energy is slower and denser whereas higher thought energy is faster and lighter. Emotionally speaking, you can easily pick up whether one is transmitting slow, dense thought energy or fast, light thought energy. Pay attention to this concept when you meet a friend, and you'll come to your own conclusions. Happy people will "feel" more light than depressed people. Passion will feel faster and lighter in your body than apathy. Notice how dense and heavy or light you're feeling now, and see if you can make a connection with both the active emotion and the thoughts running through your mind. We'll talk more about emotions and their influence on your life as well as how they are connected to thought power in Chapter 4. For now, I want you to see that outer experiences all originate from inner experiences. And if you could start making the connection that you play in a great game of life that exists in both the outer, visible world and the invisible inner world, then you're already on the way to that first breakthrough.

## Chapter 3

# Myths and Things That Get in the Way of Your Manifesting

*"Whatever you hold in your mind on a consistent basis is exactly what you will experience in your life."*

— Tony Robbins

Manifesting is a real thing. You're manifesting things all day, every day, without realizing it. Sometimes, your manifestations are instantaneous—for instance, when you think of a friend or relative you haven't seen in a while, and later that day, they call. Other times, you experience an event, and you assume it was random because your brain doesn't remember you set this particular event in motion in the form of a thought.

Then there are those times when you think about something obsessively, e.g., money or romance, and you assume you're not manifesting. Yet, if we were to investigate the contents of your thoughts around that topic, we'd find you're constantly thinking about how much you don't have that romantic partner or money. In this case, you are manifesting; it's just that you're getting more of what you don't want rather than what you'd really want. Universal laws have no sense of humor, and while they can seem tricky at times, the truth is, they are never at fault. They simply serve us more of who we've signaled we are through our thought patterns and emotions.

Thoughts really do become things. Are you starting to see that now? This is how the law of attraction operates, and it never fails. It is a ceaseless, immutable, incorruptible law. Of course, knowing that the law is at work won't benefit us if our actions are negative in nature. So, it's time to explore some of the myths and blind spots that might be creating the mismatch in your experiences.

# Myth #1:

## All you have to do is think about what you want, affirm it, and it will manifest.

The film *The Secret* is partly responsible for creating confusion around the workings of the law of attraction. Most people who watched that scene where the little boy got his dream bike assumed all they had to do was think it and *poof*, like magic, the thing would appear. When that didn't happen, they sought something more. Gurus say you need to stay positive and use affirmations morning and night, and then you will get what you want. The same people who struggled to find success after watching *The Secret* still struggle to manifest their desires even after overdosing on affirmations. What gives?

Well, I hate to break it to you, but this idea is a myth. The law of attraction doesn't give you what you want simply because you spit our great affirmative words and think about your desire. It matches you up based on vibration, not words! Go back to the chapter on the laws of success and reread how the law of vibration works if you're still having a hard time with this myth.

The truth is, it's not enough to think or write or speak about what you want. Yes, that's an important step to take in the manifestation process, but in many ways, it's the easy part that happens naturally when you're in love with this new idea or desire. However, the work you're required to do is to raise your vibrational state and open yourself to receive the good you've asked for.

# Myth #2:

## Affirmations work like magic.

Affirmations are positive statements that describe a desired state of being or a situation. But affirmations only work if feelings and thoughts are a perfect match. So, for example, if you're affirming "I am rich," but you're feeling poor and unworthy, you'll get more of what you're feeling, not what you're declaring.

So before you start blaming affirmations for your lack of manifestation, ask yourself, does my heart agree with this statement 100%? If not, why is that? Where is the doubt within me, and what is it rooted in? Be willing to do the work first to align thoughts and feelings, and don't worry too much about affirmations.

# Myth #3:

## You have to focus on the law of attraction to make it work.

This is a common misconception that new personal development students encounter. Action is necessary for the process of manifestation, and you will need to involve your mind power. However, attention and energy should not be spent on trying to control or "do" the law of attraction in any way, shape, or form.

Let me ask you this. Do you deliberately control or force the law of gravity to hold you in place as you sit on your chair for dinner? When you go out for a job, do you invest your energy in monitoring and trying to manage gravity so you don't float up into the sky? Of course not! You probably thought that was the most ridiculous analogy ever. Then, why assume you need to micromanage and control the law of attraction with your mind power?

The truth is, the law of vibration is already taking care of that. Your focus should never be on the law itself but on your feelings and actions.

# Myth #4:

## Law of attraction only works for some people.

The only people who believe this myth haven't yet received their desires. Usually, these people go around preaching that it doesn't work or isn't real merely because they haven't seen the outcome they wanted.

Let's bust this myth by reiterating that the law of attraction isn't a man-made law that can be muted or corrupted in any way. If it works for one person, it will work for all people. Nature does not discriminate, and just as gravity will work for both a holy priest and the worst criminal in the world in precisely the same way, realize that LOA is under the same universal obligation to work for you at all times.

Sometimes it may seem as though LOA isn't working. For instance, you may complain a lot about your spouse, your poor health, your awful boss, or how much you hate your job. One day, you decide to "do" the law of attraction practices for a few minutes each day before heading out into the world and jumping right back into your regular habits. Months go by, and you still don't see any desired improvement. If anything, the thing you're complaining about only seems to be getting worse. In such instances, it's easy to assume the law isn't working, but the truth is, it's working perfectly. Instead of giving you what you claim you want, it's giving you more of what you're in harmony with. Complaining and fault-finding or feeling sorry for yourself only match you up with more of what you're focused on. When you let go of this myth and start noticing what's manifesting every day, then connect it back to your most dominant thoughts, feelings, and habits, you will have the needed insight to make drastic changes.

# Myth #5:

## The law of attraction makes people greedy and self-centered.

This is a dangerous myth to entertain because it supposes so many unlawful ideas. First, it implies that having desires is bad or will turn you into a bad person. It also implies that you'll become uncaring and greedy by getting what you want. Both these ideas are false and only reveal a mind that doesn't yet understand the laws of life. When you come to an accurate understanding of the first law discussed (divine oneness), you will realize that a human being fully awakened to their spiritual and physical potential can never operate from a place of greed.

Greed is rooted in fear and lack. Knowledge of the laws of success and the practice of these laws bring forth prosperity. A mind that can manifest prosperity is a mind rooted in love and abundance. Otherwise, those riches will quickly disappear. So, when you see a man or woman manifesting wealth over and over and passing it on to the next generation, you're looking at someone with an abundant mindset, and that mindset can never be rooted in greed. The more an abundant mindset has, the more it seeks to give.

Real students and practitioners of the law of attraction become more giving, compassionate, and altruistic even as they go about manifesting their own desires.

## Myth #6:

**The law of attraction gives you whatever you visualize.**

This is another common thought, especially for people who really like selling vision boards. Visualization indeed plays an important role in training your mind to attract, but it's not the visualization itself that's manifesting, you know?

You can buy the most expensive vision board and fill it with the most luxurious items. That doesn't mean you'll manifest these things. If, like John Assaraf, you really want a new home and spend all your time picturing this dream home of yours and seeing it in vivid detail in your mind, but you do nothing else, you're still not getting that house! Why? Is visualization a lie? Not at all.

Visualizing something does help reign in your thoughts and enable you to focus on what you want the most. We think in pictures, so if I say, think about your mom, or if I called her name, you wouldn't see the letters MOM in your mind; you'd see your mother's beautiful face. Similarly, if you know you desire a new home for your family, having a picture enables you to concentrate on the right thing. But even more important are your beliefs and emotions around that "dream home" as they determine your vibrational frequency and, in turn, your ability to match up with that dream home through the LOA.

Turning thoughts into concrete reality requires way more than visualization. This book shows you what those requirements are and how to apply yourself to actualize your desires. Speaking of beliefs and emotions, let's talk about how they affect your magnetic field and, in so doing, your ability to attract what you desire.

# Chapter 4

## *Emotions, Beliefs, and Attraction*

*"The law of attraction states that whatever you focus on, think about, read about, and talk about intensely, you're going to attract more of into your life."*

— Jack Canfield

D o you know why manifesting desires is so hard for the masses? Most people are unknowingly self-sabotaging. Their emotions and beliefs get in the way of their actualization, and in the end, the law of attraction works against their desired outcome rather than for it. Lucky for you, this unconscious self-sabotaging pattern will no longer run amok in your world because, by the time you're done reading this book, you'll have the awareness and tools to help you get out of your own way.

You see, the law of attraction is ever operational, and it's there to make things easier, orderly, and predictable. If you could just flip the switch that enables you to make choices in harmony with the laws of success, everything would get easier. Well, there's no single switch to flip for an instant solution, but there are a handful of things you need to do that will, in effect, act as a switch. Over time, you will see the results of your good work. So, instead of approaching LOA with the need for a switch that works with the snap of a finger (a mistake many people make), I encourage you to approach LOA like a gardener.

## Your Mind Is Where the Game of Life Is Played

The laws of the universe, including the law of attraction, don't operate at the level of your physical realm but rather the mental and psychological realms. The real game and the creative process all take place in the mind. To tame and conquer your mind is to tame and conquer your reality because everything made manifest in the material world was first nurtured and incubated in the mind until it crystallized into form. And the mind is more like a garden than anything else in which you are the gardener, and the thoughts you entertain take hold in the soil after which they develop and grow into their kind. If you plant weeds, then your garden will be full of weeds; if you plant a rose bush, then you'll get a rose bush. If you allow weeds to take hold in your garden, it won't be too long before they destroy your rose bush because weeds are notorious for hogging all the nutrients.

In a practical sense, this is the bulk of the work you must do. A mind with infertile soil and plenty of weeds cannot produce a beautiful garden. And the law of attraction will serve that garden to create more of whatever dominates. Your emotions and beliefs come into play to help you become a successful gardener with the best products. The more you can work on these emotions and beliefs, the less likely you will sabotage your manifestations. Why? To understand that concept, we need to learn what emotions and beliefs are and their role in the creative process within an individual.

# What Are Emotions?

Merriam Webster defines an emotion as "a conscious mental reaction (such as anger or fear) subjectively experienced as strong feeling usually directed toward a specific object and typically accompanied by physiological and behavioral changes in the body." A more straightforward way of defining emotion is thinking of it as the conscious awareness of your vibrational state. It's how your conscious mind knows what's going on in your subconscious mind and the signals you're transmitting. And since we are vibrational beings ever communicating with our environment and the universe through vibration, your emotional state is a huge deal. How you feel is what the law of attraction responds to at all times. So, if your emotions are out of sync with your desire, you'll find yourself on the negative side of the manifestation, i.e., lack of the thing desired. I'm going to show you how to use your emotions properly, but before that, let's also define beliefs.

# What Are Beliefs?

A belief is anything you've assumed is truth. Your beliefs of yourself determine the results you get in life—did you know that? The thoughts and ideas you entertain and affirm as true (even if they are not fundamental truths) are stored as your beliefs. They become your set-point and the framework through which you approach life. You inherit some of your beliefs from your parents, who inherited them from their parents. Some have developed over time as you experienced life. Not all of those views are harmful, but if you're having trouble in a specific area of your life, there's a belief you need to change. Until you can become aware of and examine both your beliefs and dominant emotional states, not much else can change.

## You Have an Inner GPS

If you own a car, you're already familiar with a GPS; it's a guidance technology that helps you reach your desired destination. Even if you've never been to that new place, if you follow the instructions and stay on course, the GPS will get you there. Start to think of your emotions as a GPS because they are there to guide you. When you become aware of a negative emotion, the proper response should never be suppression, self-loathing, or more guilt for having that emotion; instead, you should see the negative emotion as a sign that you're off-track in both thought and vibrational transmission. If you got a signal from your vehicle's GPS informing you that you made a wrong turn, you wouldn't stop the car and wallow in self-pity, would you? Of course not. You'd simply find the next best exit and reroute the car, then be on your way. With emotions, this is precisely what you need to do: recognize and label that unpleasant emotion, process it, and consciously reroute your mental energy so you can get back to the desired emotional state. The critical thing is to first learn what different emotions represent on the vibrational scale. It's straightforward, and Abraham Hicks did a good job creating an emotional guidance scale to help everyone grasp how much they would need to reroute before getting back to those pleasant high-frequency states.

## Do you always need to keep rerouting? Isn't being happy all the time unrealistic?

It's not a matter of being happy all the time; instead, it's about reaching for the next best feeling you can find. By default, the laws of nature will land you on those lower vibrations as you go through life. When that natural law of polarity and the law of rhythm land you in a less-than-pleasing season of stress, difficulties, and unwanted news, you'll need a way of processing corresponding emotions and the ability to keep reaching for a better feeling. That's the only way to stay on your path and move into a new reality. While negative emotions such as fear, anger, and powerlessness do have their place in the human experience, their vibrational frequency is pretty dense. They make positive manifestations challenging because their vibration is way off-route relative to the frequency of a positive manifestation. So, how do you effectively use your emotions and the guidance they give?

## Here's a Simple Formula

Right thought + Right emotions + Right behavior and action = Desired outcome.

That means you need to make sure the quality of your emotion is in sync with whatever objective you want to manifest. For example, let's say Christine has a burning desire to remarry again, but this time with her soulmate. Finding true love is a beautiful desire to have, and Christine feels like she's never experienced such love before. Her relationships have probably been primarily at a lower frequency, yet she wants to attract and manifest a high-frequency relationship. Christine needs to boost her magnetic powers and raise her vibrational frequency around love and relationships to manifest this desire. She will need to consistently transmit signals that the law of attraction can respond to in due time.

So, Christine always maintains the proper thought, high vibrating emotions, and takes the right action. Various techniques and strategies enable her to accomplish this without strain, and as you get into the later parts of this book, you'll get to learn what strategies will boost your magnetic powers, too.

But suppose Christine isn't aware of these strategies. Instead of using the above formula, she quickly falls into and gets stuck on lower frequencies of anger, self-doubt, powerlessness, hopelessness, and thinking true love it can't happen for her because she's too old or not loveable enough. In that case, her behavior and actions will match those emotions, and regardless of her desire for true love or her attempts to meet someone, her desired outcome will remain out of reach. Even if she "forces" the situation by asking friends to set her up with any man they know, the law of attraction would only match her up with a man who vibrates at that lower frequency, not that high-frequency soulmate.

Is the law of attraction capricious? Absolutely not. Christine is the one determining whom she is ready to be matched with. Based on her dominant emotions and behavior (despite the clues from her emotional GPS), Christine is operating at a vibrational level that's not in sync with her claim of true love.

We often make this mistake with money, love, and health. If you have a burning desire that hasn't manifested no matter how hard you tried, you're likely making the same mistake. As we start to talk about how LOA works in the next chapter, you'll get step-by-step suggestions of what to do to stop getting in the way of your manifestations.

## The Abraham Hicks Emotional Guidance Scale

According to Abraham Hicks, the emotional guidance scale helps you identify your vibration. This scale lays them out from positive emotions at the highest level to negative emotions at the lower end, and everything in between. The premise is that the closer you are to joy, the higher your vibrational frequency, and the further you are from joy, the lower your vibration.

1. Joy/Appreciation/Empowerment/Freedom/Love
2. Passion
3. Enthusiasm/Eagerness/Happiness
4. Positive Expectation
5. Optimism
6. Hopefulness
7. Contentment
8. Boredom
9. Pessimism
10. Frustration/Irritation/Impatience
11. Overwhelment (feeling overwhelmed)
12. Disappointment
13. Doubt
14. Worry
15. Blame
16. Discouragement (feeling discouraged)
17. Anger
18. Revenge
19. Hatred/Rage
20. Jealousy
21. Insecurity/Guilt/Unworthiness
22. Fear/Grief/Desperation/Despair/Powerlessness

## How to Use This Scale as a Tool for Boosting Your Manifesting Powers

With this list of commonly experienced emotions, you can identify where you are at any given point of your day and deliberately move higher up the scale. Choose to reach for a better-feeling thought, and once you're there, work on stabilizing that thought before moving up to the next emotion. It's a practice that takes time, patience, and self-compassion, but once you get into it, you'll enjoy the ability to dictate how you want to feel at any given moment. And the best part is, you'll definitely understand the signals your GPS gives you as you go about your day. Anytime you start to mess with your manifestations, you'll get a ping telling you that you're not feeling good. If you realize you're too far down in that scale, don't attempt to shoot up to joy just because you know that's where you need to be. Instead, gently guide yourself back up there by climbing that stair-case as you would a typical staircase in the physical world. One step at a time, one foot in front of the other. That's what makes this tool effective and what enables you to finally become a master of your emotions and, in turn, your manifestations.

# Chapter 5

## *How the Law of Attraction Works*

*"If you see it in your mind, you'll hold it in your hand."*

— Bob Proctor

Consider for a moment the process of childbirth. A woman will conceive and carry a tiny (but growing) fetus for about nine months before the being is introduced into the physical world as a human baby. The entire development and nurturing of the single cell into a complete human takes place within the woman, utterly invisible to us. We've learned to trust that nature knows what it's doing, and as long we do the bare minimum, the results are guaranteed.

Your manifestation requires a similar understanding. To create the life of your dreams, you'll need to play from the inside out. Your manifestations have their origin, incubation, and entire nurture cycle taking place within you first, just as we see with a pregnant woman.

And like everything else in nature, your desire goes through gestation. It needs time to form and transform before that final outer manifestation occurs. If at any time during your "pregnancy," you miscarry, you won't have the pleasure of turning thoughts into things. How long does it take for your desire to turn into full manifestation? That is both a complex and easy question to answer. In the animal kingdom, we know it takes about nine months for human pregnancy and about twenty-two months for an elephant, but the length of your desire's gestation is a little more challenging to estimate accurately. It might be a day, week, month, year, or longer. You need to learn and cultivate certain things to foster the best environment for faster manifestations (you'll learn more about these ideas in chapter 8). You will also need to give up or eliminate certain things from your mental, emotional, and spiritual diet if you want to avoid self-sabotage, AKA miscarriage, during the manifesting process. Those you'll learn about in-depth in chapter 7. By letting go of what doesn't serve you and doing more of what does, your manifestation pattern will gradually become clear. In other words, how long it takes depends on you and the things you do and don't do.

# How Real Is Your Reality?

Most of us have the deeply held belief that reality is fixed. We assume everyone experiences life the way we do. If that's your deeply held belief, it will be hard to see positive changes in your life. Two people can experience the same traumatic event, yet one will transform and emerge better than ever before, and the other will succumb to deep depression, never recovering from that trauma. What gives? Our perception of what is "real"—that is, whatever you believe is real for you—must become the only thing that is real.

One of the most powerful things you can do right now if you're serious about aligning with your desires is to ask yourself a few simple questions:

#1: Do I believe life is working for me or against me?

#2: Am I born to be a victim or a conqueror in the story of my life?

#3: How much of my reality is fixed, and how much of my thinking is plastic?

The founder of Mindvalley, Vishen Lakhiani, coined the term "bending reality," which he believes is the secret behind the world's most successful and influential manifesters. Lakhiani has traveled the globe interviewing all kinds of people, from billionaires to spiritual masters living in the mountains, and the one thing he banks on is the fact that we've got it all wrong. We are meant to bend reality to our will, not succumb to it like victims. Will Smith has echoed similar sentiments in the past; he's publicly said that he knows the universe is like water, and it will move and mold itself to the individual's mind if they know what they're doing; that's how he's been able to create his dream lifestyle. And in case you're still thinking, "This is still just guru opinions and nothing based on hard proof," allow me to share some insights from experts on the subject of reality, higher consciousness, and science.

Deepak Chopra, MD says:

*Imagine someone sitting in a chair wearing state-of-the-art virtual reality gear. In the simulation bombarding his senses, he's racing in the Indy 500, running away from tigers in the jungle, or walking a tightrope. These are perilous adventures that he is immersed in, where survival itself is at stake. His body will exhibit all the signs of a stress response. But his experience is entirely fake, a construct by clever VR engineers. This imaginary setup is what occurs to all of us in daily life. We inhabit a virtual reality that's so powerful it blinds us to the truth. What we accept as real is mind-made, but when you are inside this spell/illusion/dream, your struggles totally envelop you.*

— (Chopra, 2020)

In short, just because your current mind-made reality feels like the only real thing, that doesn't mean you should buy into it. Learn to recognize the difference between fundamental truth and perceptual/mind-made reality.

Going back to Vishen, not only is he spreading this message on social media (just check out Lakhiani's Facebook post from August 3, 2019), but he is also working on a formula that he thinks can work for anyone. It's still a work in progress, but the main idea resonates with me because it involves having clear self-identity, intuition, clarity, bliss, and a strong mission. It's also about putting in the effort, i.e., taking action, but the right kind of action and, last but not least, eliminating negativity. Are you starting to see that you're not stuck in your current reality? If you can allow that possibility to sink in, you've done the all-important job of priming yourself for the next chapter, where we take the first critical step in the process of manifesting.

## How You're Getting What You're Getting (It's Not Random)

Ours is an orderly universe governed by laws that work in perfect precision. None of your significant manifestations are ever random; you simply forgot when you planted the initial seed in your mind. Heck, the seeds might have been planted by your parents long before you could think for yourself, and now you're reaping the consequences of the cause set in motion. On the one hand, this notion can be quite disheartening because it places you squarely as the one responsible for your reality, but on the other hand, it can be liberating. As the person in charge of the effects and quality of your life, you can initiate a new chain of causation, cancel out the current cycle, and find yourself in a completely new reality. After all, if perceptual reality is all mind-made, why choose to go on experiencing a terrible aspect of it when you could just as easily be enjoying a more pleasant mind-made construct?

If I can think back to the example Chopra used about the VR game, the player was in danger, struggling to survive, even though he was probably sitting on a chair in his bedroom wearing winter pajamas. I'd say we need to figure out how to make our "game" of reality more enjoyable and better suited to our unique preferences. What you consider fun might be completely miserable for me, and vice versa. So, the trick isn't to create a copy-paste perceptual reality, but rather to work on identifying what's right for our individuality. When you "play the game" you were born to play, two crucial things that will happen simultaneously: first, you'll naturally begin to align with the laws of life; second, your ability to magnetize more desired experiences increases.

# Increasing Your Magnetic Power

Years ago, before I worked on myself and increased my magnetic powers, I had a relative whom I always wanted to be around. Each time he came to visit, I'd spend all my time trying to figure out what made him so attractive to success. I noticed he would tell my parents about his latest business idea, and almost immediately, he'd manifest it and succeed. My mom used to say, "He's got the Midas touch," and I would think, "Man, I'd like to have that too."

Imagine for a moment having that same power. Would you like to be featured in *Vogue* magazine or get a branding deal with your favorite brand? All you have to do is speak it to life, and it manifests. Would you like to meet your soulmate? Declare it, and tomorrow during your morning run, afternoon grocery shopping, or while searching for parking outside your favorite restaurant, you'll bump into that person you've always dreamed of.

It's easy to spot people who can naturally speak and immediately manifest their ideas. Most of the time, they don't even know how they do it, so it makes it hard to pass on the same secret to others. These individuals are not any more special than you and me;

they are highly charged, positive magnets, and that's something anyone can learn to do with a little deliberate practice.

But before I share with you how to charge yourself positively, let's acknowledge how being a highly charged magnet can be both positive and negative. In other words, you could be someone who often manifests negative experiences. For example, you might say, " I always miss the bus" or "I always get stuck in traffic on my way to the airport, and it creates a lot of stress." Invariably, each time you try to catch the bus or the plane, you'll experience that frustration. In my LOA community, a new member told us about how he would move from one abusive relationship to the next. Since childhood, women in his life have always taken advantage of him in horrible ways. He seems to be "cursed," as he said, but really, what he didn't know was that he was a powerful magnet for women who didn't have his best interest at heart.

Therefore, as you think of magnetism, make sure you point your intention and attention in a positive direction. Life is impersonal; just as weeds will grow abundantly in the same soil as the most beautiful roses, unwanted experiences can be drawn to you just as quickly as wanted.

Positively charging yourself isn't rocket science. It could happen naturally and with the least amount of effort, provided your beliefs, habits, and thought patterns are constructive. So, here's what you need to do: work on your energy and focus all your attention on the existing good and the increase that you begin to notice. Build up your energy with high-frequency thoughts and emotions so you can create a positive energy field around you. Leverage this energy every moment of the day, especially while at work or applying for a job. In practical terms, if you desire to earn $20k each month and you've never been able to realize that goal, the way to become magnetic is to focus all your attention on the income you currently have. When you look at your bank account, wallet, or purse, focus on what is currently there and what you were able to produce this month, and let that energy be the most dominant one. If you can earn one dollar, surely you can earn a million. The law of attraction doesn't know the difference in quantity; it only reads the vibrational signal. The same is true if you're looking to manifest a healthy lean body or a relationship. To be magnetic to more good, start with the good you currently have and use it as fuel to stabilize you in that higher vibrational frequency.

# What If I Have Nothing Good Going for Me?

I've had plenty of people tell me, "You don't understand, bro. I'm broke, unemployed, and I have child support to pay. My wallet is empty, so how can I feel good about money right now?" If you feel that way, the solution is simple. Stop looking at your finances and find another area in your life where you're currently creating positive manifestations. The great trick the ego plays on us is this idea of segregation; that is, we think things are separate from each other. For example, we believe our relationships, health, attitudes, and view of the world have nothing to do with how successful our business endeavor becomes. The truth is, oneness is all there is, and everything is connected. So, when you do something evil to someone, thinking no one can see it, the negative consequences of that action show up in places you wouldn't have thought possible. In that same light, when we do or feel good in one area of our life, that positivity is passed to areas we wouldn't have expected. So, maybe that broke dad cannot kickstart his magnetism by looking at his current financial situation because things are bleak. But you know what? I bet if he looked carefully, he might realize he's currently enjoying the best health of his life. Maybe his relationship with his kid has become exceptionally great, or perhaps that little garden patch he started working on a few months ago has gone from barren desert to a beautiful Garden of Eden, giving him plenty of organic veggies and making it easier for him to eat well despite the financial constraints he's facing. These are all examples of areas where he is already a positive magnet. His job is to deliberately focus on amplifying that positivity until it fills up most of his day; then, he can go about looking for job interviews and looking for gigs that can help him get back on his feet. If he sustains that high-frequency vibration and builds up his energetic field to be predominantly positive, the law of attraction would unfailingly deliver new results. That is the law.

# Chapter 6

## *Desire as the First Step*

*"Man, alone, has the power to transform his thoughts into physical reality; man, alone, can dream and make his dreams come true."*

— Napoleon Hill

Everyone approaches manifestation differently, but one commonality among all successful manifestors (including famous celebrities like Oprah and Jim Carrey) is that they all begin with total clarity about what they want. In other words, they start by identifying their desire.

Napoleon Hill wrote:

*The starting point of all achievement is desire...
Every human being who reaches the age of understanding of the purpose of money wishes for it.
Wishing will not bring riches. But desiring riches
with a state of mind that becomes an obsession, then
planning definite ways and means to acquire riches
and backing those plans with persistence which
does not recognize failure will bring riches.*

— (Hill, Think And Grow Rich,
1937)

That's why it's time for you to decide what you really, really want. What do you desire to be, do, or have more of? What does your heart genuinely ache for?

This moment is when you should begin to realign yourself and work with the laws. Before you can dive into and implement the tactics and techniques known to accelerate manifestation, this part must become extra-clear in your mind. You need to create a blueprint your mind can work with henceforth because as you know, manifestation begins in the mind. The foundation of that manifestation (think of it as a seed that you plant if the gardener analogy resonates, or as a blueprint if you prefer to see yourself as an architect of your life) depends on the work you do before moving on to subsequent chapters.

# Origin of Desire

There are different desires, some of which are purely physical, others are emotional, and others are spiritual. When you're hungry, you have a physical desire; however, sometimes it can be a craving, which would make the desire both emotional and physical (e.g., when you crave your favorite ice cream). Most of the desires that lead you to pick up this book are likely spiritual desires coming from your higher self. When a desire emerges from within, you don't want to jump on the first impulse you get because at that point, the image in your mind isn't clear enough. Your ego might be misreading some of the information you're downloading from your higher self.

For instance, you might desire to start your own thriving business and become an impactful social entrepreneur driving positive change in the community. But at the moment, you might be working a job that brings you very little fulfillment because it's not in any way related to social impact. As that burning desire grows, your ego might fixate on the fact that you hate your job, boss, etc., and cause you to take action that may not necessarily lead you to the deep-seated desire. That's not ideal. If, however, you invest time working out your mental blueprint to figure out what that inner urge is, you'd have clarity of mind. And you'd soon realize that what you long for is to work for yourself in a business that helps the community. The action steps surrounding that new awareness would be totally different, don't you agree? Perhaps you might even stay at your current job longer as you put into place the necessary resources and support to help you execute your desire.

I hope you're seeing where I'm going with this. Having clarity about the desire enables you to focus on the right things. And where attention goes, energy flows.

## Isn't Desire Selfish?

Many religions and various schools of thought have conditioned the population to believe that desiring something is selfish and evil. I suppose this deeply rooted belief is one we all have to contend with—much like we need to deal with the topic of money and whether it's wrong to be rich or sex and whether it should only be enjoyed by married couples. If these are beliefs active in your mind, that's something you need to reconcile first. I can share my perspective and what other modern spiritual leaders have shared. I believe desires are divine seeds that enable us to unlock our fullest potential. A burning desire will always be good for both the individual and the world around them in some way, shape, or form; otherwise, it doesn't qualify as a genuine desire. Sometimes, we confuse superficial cravings and envy with desire—these are not the same. If you want to manifest a car because you're trying to keep up with the Joneses, I wouldn't consider that a desire.

Deepak Chopra says, "Desires are seeds waiting for their season to sprout. From a single seed of desire, whole forests grow. Desire is what leads you through life until the time comes when you desire a higher life. So do not be ashamed that you want so much, yet at the same time, do not fool yourself into thinking that what you want today will be enough tomorrow."

Give yourself permission to uncover the seeds that are now ready to come to fruition. Pay attention and get extremely clear on what you want and why you desire it. The more clarity you have, the better your positive magnetic power. If there's more than one burning desire, that's okay. Open up your private journal or notebook and make a list of all the burning desires. As you write down your list, be mindful of the words you choose. For example, if you desire a healthy body and you're currently going through health challenges, make sure you write "I desire a healthy body," not "I desire to stop being sick." Can you sense the difference? Writing down your desires and goals in the positive (what you want) instead of the negative is critical in the manifesting process. Once you've detailed the desire as vividly as possible and painted the complete picture of the experience you have, it's time to pinpoint the goals surrounding that desire and make a plan. But what if you're unable to identify a burning desire?

## I Don't Know What I Want

If you're sitting there thinking "*I don't think I know what I want,*" you're not alone. Not everyone discovers their desire and purpose at age nine. Some people work hard and hustle all their lives, chasing after things they were told they should want, and at fifty years old, they finally realize they don't really know what their true desire is. If you're unsure how to figure out what you really want, start by looking in some unusual places. For example, make a list of the things you really don't like and what you most fear. Fear and hatred are strong indicators and carry a lot of insights for us. You can also take note of the things you're jealous of because anytime you're jealous, that emotion is telling you there's something you want, but you're afraid to claim it. Another unusual place to look is where you've experienced the greatest suffering, pain, or failure.

Once you've made a list of all these different so-called negative things, start writing their opposite next to them. While these negative things can be highly uncomfortable, they often act as the disguise containing that seed of desire that will unlock a version of ourselves we didn't know was there. For example, if you've struggled with weight all your life and you hate how fat you feel, the opposite of fat is optimum health and ideal body weight.

As you can see, it's okay to start with what you don't like. Check out the chapter on techniques you can use to align with the law of attraction. An exercise titled "Clarity through Contrast" will enable you to identify your true desire. Follow the steps in this exercise and identify each negative situation. Now, identify the new positive desire that thrills and amplifies your energy. The stronger the electric current, the better. Repeat this exercise as many times as needed until you find the thing that makes you come alive—that's the desire to go for.

## Don't Hold Yourself Back

While it might seem logical to play small or go for a desire that seems more realistic, know that this is the worst way to exercise your creative power. It also won't help you increase your attraction factor. You are far more than a human being, and your ability to dream, desire, and work toward the realization of your chosen desires is your destiny. So, stop holding yourself back. When picking your desire, think big; get absolutely thrilled and filled with joy. Find something worth living for, and you will automatically summon the creative energy from the universe that's ready and willing to bring forth your greatest desires. Allow yourself to go after this big exciting thing and take this next step.

We've taken the first step and initiated manifestation. Make a commitment to yourself that you'll go all the way and give it your all. Once you've made this commitment, your subconscious mind will start generating ideas, emotions, and behaviors that move you into the right kind of action.

More on that later. For now, the only thing to do is first identify what you want, and why. Once you've done that, make a binding commitment and let the divine forces in your life get to work, prepping the necessary resources, opportunities, and people essential in realizing this desire.

Let's move on.

# Chapter 7

## *What Makes Manifesting Your Dream Life So Hard?*

*"Most people are thinking about what they don't want, and they're wondering why it shows up over and over again."*

— John Assaraf

Once you've identified your desire, established clear goals, and practiced affirmations, you should manifest what you want, right? Not quite. The creative process is simple, the laws are unfailing in theory, and manifesting is straightforward. Observe nature, and you'll see how effortless evolution, growth, and manifestation are.

But we need to realize that simple rarely means easy in the context of human experience. Why? Because human beings are highly complex. As such, manifesting whatever you want is determined by how well you're managing your complexities. We'll discuss the various aspects of being human that might create blocks, delays, and even cancel out desires. But before we get to that, let's clarify what manifesting means to ensure our aligned perspectives.

So, what is manifesting exactly?

Manifesting is the creative process through which an idea turns into a burning desire and takes shape in the material world as something that can be experienced in some way, shape, or form. It begins with a concept in your mind and comes to completion as an experienced result in the material world. Better said, it's how the divine, invisible substance takes visible form.

Everything you see in our world consists of concepts materialized from the cars we drive, the homes we live in, the food we eat, and the clothes we wear. Health is a manifestation, and so is disease. Money is also a manifestation, and so is poverty. All the advancements of modern civilization came about because someone, somewhere, initiated manifesting through thought and a burning desire. Both pleasant and unpleasant manifestations follow the same creative process.

Suppose you want to have different experiences in life. In that case, you need to learn how to direct your manifesting powers in more constructive ways so you can have the quality of life you desire.

The majority of our population (even those who claim they don't believe in LOA or manifesting) constantly manifest on auto-pilot. That means they unconsciously go about co-creating experiences that, to them, seem random. And because they cannot direct their intention and attention, it appears that manifesting isn't real. What they affirm and write as desirable goals never come to fruition because their life runs on auto-pilot systems that are not pro-manifesting their particular desire. The main issue here isn't the autopilot system; instead, it's the fact that the system is developed well enough to positively co-create these desires.

By going through this book, you're taking yourself out of mass thinking and behavior to learn how to deliberately bring about the manifestations you desire. Suppose you want this process to be as natural and foolproof as possible. In that case, we need to look at the different aspects that might hinder the desired manifestation. The biggest and most important aspect is your belief system.

# Beliefs

Our beliefs make up the lens through which we view and experience the world. Imagine wearing black and white lenses all your life. In that case, it would be hard to believe a person who told you that the rainbow has seven bright colors or that the sun is a red star. Everything you experience would be filtered through a black and white lens, which means you'd only perceive things as black or white. Countless arguments would ensue whenever you met someone who disagreed with your perspective. If you happen to live where everyone wears the same colored lens as you, the collective verdict would be that the idiot talking about the colors of the rainbow needs medical attention.

This is the power of our belief system. Louise Hay said that our beliefs take hold at a very young age.

Subsequently, every experience we create somehow matches those beliefs. In fact, the things we hate or disagree with are only so because our belief system is in opposition with that thing.

Don't believe me? Take a moment now, close your eyes and bring to mind a few of the critical events and experiences you've had. Notice how often the same patterns repeat themselves and how often you've proven yourself right.

When the belief is progressive and constructive such as "I'm successful at everything I set my mind to," you have experiences matching that. If, however, you've made long-held agreements—aka beliefs that are limiting—then you're in trouble. Those beliefs will almost always block any progress being made toward your desire. What's crazy about limiting beliefs is they seem so natural and logical, so your reality will be filled with plenty of people, conditions, and other evidence supporting that blockage.

## So How Do We Neutralize and Transform Our Existing Limiting Beliefs?

First, we uncover the agreements and truths that keep us stuck, then we neutralize the active charge that gives them the power to sabotage our progress. Lastly, we replace the old beliefs with new ones. Pretty simple, right? While it will require practice, discipline, and a strong will to shift a belief, the effort is worthwhile. On the other side of this limiting belief is your desire.

*Exercise:*

Shake up your beliefs with this mental exercise to uncover the agreements you have relative to your desire. How do you feel when you think about manifesting your burning desire and achieving the corresponding goals? Do you think it will be hard/impossible/difficult to do? How do your beliefs make you feel? Do they make you feel small and powerless, or strong and powerful? If you notice any negative thoughts, how would you like to change them?

Write down the constructive and empowering beliefs you want to have. Start cultivating them today.

## The Results Equation

Now that you're aware of beliefs and the dangers of limiting beliefs, let's discuss the details of the manifesting process. At times, the reason for our lack of manifestation is that we don't yet understand all the moving pieces and our role in the creative process. So how do material results—whether money, a relationship, a toned and healthy body—come about? There's a simple formula you want to memorize and perhaps hang on your bathroom mirror.

> Manifesting a Result = Right Thought + Right Emotion + Behavior + Inspired Action

Your behavior and attitude determine your actions, which are likewise determined by your emotions and thought patterns. Nowhere should the action entail trying to manage the law of attraction. Instead, the action must align with the plan you set for yourself and the inner guidance you get as you move closer toward your desire.

Suppose you've been studying LOA and trying to manifest your goals purely through positive thinking. Still, you didn't follow that thinking up with the proper behavior and action. In that case, it's unlikely you'll get what you want.

A businessman recently discovered this blind spot. After years of being a personal development student, religiously following Abraham Hicks, and rewatching *The Secret* hundreds of times, he found himself slowly falling into depression. Nothing seemed to work. At first, he was optimistic when thinking about the future, and everything felt good. He was relaxed, his blood pressure went down, and he did his daily affirmations morning and night without fail. Yet over time, his optimism started waning because nothing was manifesting. By the time we got the chance to speak, he had turned from an advocate to a protestor of LOA.

After some deep conversations, he was willing to open up and share exactly what he'd been doing for the past five years. Although his desire was to expand the business and bring in some new investors, he had no definite plan, and no action was consistently applied toward that end. Therefore, the results could not please him because he'd missed critical pieces of that manifesting equation.

If you don't want to set yourself up for failure, you'll have to ensure you're working with the right manifesting formula and cultivate beliefs that support the new desire so that you can execute toward your desires.

# Other Ways We Block Manifesting Desires

## Self-Esteem

How healthy is your sense of self-esteem and sense of worth? A guy shared in our online community his struggle to find a job even though he was an excellent software engineer. He tried everything he could think of to get a job, and it was evident that his real issue was lack of confidence. Sometimes, that's the only thing standing in the way of your manifestation.

Remember, energy is everything, and despite popular belief, we all read each other's energy. When you apply for a job or approach that dream girl to ask her out (or even a new prospect to sell your product), your confidence level matters and will influence that interaction. Although the person may not consciously know it, they will not be attracted to whatever you want them to do.

Sometimes, our confidence is low because we feel like we don't deserve success, or struggle with shame and feelings of inadequacy. Whatever your reasons might be for living with an unhealthy level of self-confidence, cultivate your self-esteem and find ways to increase your sense of worth.

Self-esteem and self-confidence are intertwined with self-belief. That's why I suggest increasing your belief in yourself and your abilities. As law of attraction practitioners, we don't get what we affirm, write down every day as our goal, or what we claim we deserve; instead, we get whatever we believe is right for us. Often, when we believe something is right and true, we'll work to make that belief a reality, whether the belief is beneficial or detrimental to our wellbeing.

## Tips to Increase Both Self-Confidence and Self-Belief

### #1: Become curious and aware of the emotions you tend to experience.

Do you often struggle with self-doubt and anxiety? These emotions are powerful influencers of our perception of ourselves. When your brain tells you that "you can't" or that "you'll make a fool of yourself," these messages damage your ability to move forward with confidence. So, identify these emotions and the beliefs you have about yourself. Then, move on to the second tip as it is super important.

## #2: Identity your self-talk and silence that inner critic.

Psychologists say that most people live in an invisible, self-manufactured hell because of the inner dialogue and silent criticisms they entertain throughout the day. The stuff you tell yourself is more destructive than anything someone can say to you. An overreactive inner critic will poison and tear down any bit of self-belief you have left, and that will make it impossible for you to dream big and manifest your dreams.

Pay attention to that voice and learn to distinguish it from your higher self—the wiser, more benevolent voice that will guide you into alignment. The inner critic is often judgmental, cynical, loud, and thinks in terms of worst-case scenarios. For example, a voice might say, *"This book is silly. None of these things work and it's just another waste of time."* When you hear that, don't shun it. Instead, get curious and ask yourself, "What if it's not a waste of time? What if there's one idea in here that can help me move closer to my goals in life?"

The important thing is to slowly retrain your brain to remain open to possibility. Encourage it to consider things beyond its logical comprehension as long as those things genuinely and naturally feel good. The more you catch yourself engaging in critical self-talk and redirect that conversation to be more loving and optimistic, the easier it will be to tame that inner critic and neutralize the effects of that negative self-talk. With a lot of practice, you'll turn the inner dialogue from negative to positive, and one day, you'll wake up and realize your self-belief has exponentially grown.

## #3: Cut out negative friends and acquaintances

How many friends and acquaintances do you have who support your dreams and goals? Suppose you're hanging out with naysayers and pessimists. In that case, it's going to be tough believing you can manifest your dream life. Keeping the company of such people destroys any progress you make, so limit the amount of time you spend together, even if they are family members. If it's a spouse who treats you poorly and causes you to feel unworthy, speak to them and make it clear that you're done tolerating negativity.

In the words of Mark Twain:

> *"Keep away from people who try to belittle your ambitions. Small people always do that, but the really great make you feel that you, too, can become great."*

Find more of those great people and let them form your support structure.

## #4: Practice self-love

The foundation of healthy self-confidence and strong self-belief is self-love. That doesn't mean becoming self-centered and narcissistic; rather, it's about learning to love yourself and accept yourself for who you really are.

Many people looking to manifest love wonder why their soulmate doesn't show up no matter how hard they look. You cannot find that person who will love you unconditionally and see you for your true self if you don't do it for yourself first. It's not easy to love ourselves because society conditions us to believe we are flawed or lacking in some way. So, loving yourself will take some effort on your part, especially if you're a man. Start with small things like blocking time each week to do something you love. That can mean sitting with a book, going for a walk, getting a massage, or whatever else makes you feel special. Identify your personal values and the principles you want to live by. Own them, be proud of your deal-breakers, and never compromise those values for anything or everyone. Take note of both your strengths and weaknesses, and lean into your strengths. Do not deny your weaknesses, and you can even choose to work on them, but always remember your strengths make you more than worthy of success. So, focus on your strengths and appreciate your uniqueness.

## #5: Feed your mind the proper diet

If you want the law of attraction to match you with more of your desires, you need to go on a strict mental diet. What do you read, listen to, and watch daily? Are you seeking advice from people living the life you want to live, or from those that are stuck and unhappy? The food you give your mind is just as important as the food you give your body. If you're not eating the right kind of content, it's going to be rough. So, I want you to consider watching documentaries about people who have done great things in life. Invest in the education that will enable you to grow in the area you want to change. For example, if your desire is money, not only should you have a definite plan of how to earn more, but you should also learn about finance, money management, and anything else money-related that will increase your sense of competency. The more competent your brain feels, the easier it will be to believe in yourself because your brain knows you've put in the work and developed new skills.

## Chapter 8

# *The Real Secret to Building Your Dream Life*

*"I believe in manifestation. I believe in putting a rocket of desire out in the universe. You get it when you believe you have it. People still sit around and go 'When it's gonna come, when it's gonna come.' And that's the wrong way. You're facing away from it. You have to go, 'It's here, it's here, it's here.'"*

— Jim Carrey

"A s a man thinketh in his heart, so is he." These famous words have become commonplace quotes on social media. Still, they possess significant meaning for law of attraction practitioners because we know that manifesting our dream life is more than just affirmations and positive thinking. In fact, these techniques won't work if our thought patterns oppose our desire.

This chapter will focus on three key things: deliberate creation, intention, and allowing. The real secret to co-creating your dream life is to understand these spiritual principles contained within the law of attraction.

Let's begin with the spiritual law of deliberate creation.

# The Art and Science of Deliberate Creation

Understanding and applying the law of deliberate creation is both an art and a science because it requires calculated moves while at the same time allowing enough room for play and flexibility. In its simplest form, it's about becoming more aware and deliberate about where you put your attention. Anyone or anything that takes up your energy, thoughts, and emotions becomes your point of attraction, whether negative or positive. The more emotionally charged and prolonged a thought, the faster you will attract more things that are a vibrational match.

Consider for a moment a time in your life when you felt extremely happy and thrilled. If you left your house in the morning ecstatic that day, things just seemed to add onto that joyful state, right? Perhaps all the traffic lights were green, and that irritating traffic you usually have to deal with wasn't there. Someone at work said something wonderful to you, and perhaps a friend offered to pay for your lunch.

Now, think about a time when you were grumpy from the moment you stepped out of bed and consider how that day went.

When we take a step back to observe how life plays out, we start to see that every day seems to have a "theme," and events, people, and experiences seem to pile on to match that theme of the day. To understand the practical applications of deliberate creation, you need to wear both artistic and scientific hats. First, you want to investigate your current dominant theme. Do you just wake up and allow conditions to dictate what your "theme of the day" will be? If so, then you're likely just falling from one seemingly random event to another. On days when the theme is positive, then you get more positivity into your life. On days when it's negative, you feel powerless and victimized by life.

Investigate and take notes for about seven days to spot your patterns, then choose to wear a playfully artistic perspective and become deliberate about how you go through life. Just as an artist starts with a blank canvas, see each day as your blank canvas and commit to creating your theme of the day.

The law of deliberate creation only requires you to have the will and desire to choose what you want to experience. Choose your dominant emotional state and the thoughts you entertain. Suppose you got this book so you could improve finances and manifest wealth. In that case, you will need to become more deliberate about the emotions and thoughts you choose to dwell on as you go about your day. This act is even more important if you work in a job you can't stand. If you're still stuck in poverty and a victim mindset, feeling powerless and fearful about the economy, then it doesn't matter how many law of attraction books you read. Nothing will change on the outside because: "As a man thinketh in his heart, so is he."

To tame your thinking patterns and become more deliberate about your daily experiences, you need to cultivate certain habits. That's where intention plays a big role. In fact, the law of deliberate creation only works when you get better at consciously setting the right intentions and sticking to them throughout the day.

# The Power of Intention (Setting Intentions)

Intentions are the driving force behind our perception and experience of reality on a day-to-day basis. They are the keys to manifesting your dream life because when you're backed by a firm intention, you can consciously direct your thoughts and emotions to stay focused on what you want rather than what you don't want. With the right intentions, you'll be grounded in the energy that fulfills desires.

## How do I set the right intention for manifesting?

First, you need to list what you want to manifest. If you haven't done so yet, now is the time. Once you have written your list on a paper or card that's easy to carry around, get into the habit of looking at your list before you sleep and first thing in the morning.

The second thing you need to do is detach yourself. This one might be a bit tricky if you haven't studied the law of detachment so keep reading the book because we'll dive deeper into detachment later in the book. For now, realize that to manifest a burning desire, there's a delicate, playful dance you need to perform. On the one hand, you must hold your obsessive passion over that desire; on the other, you must surrender and detach so your emotions remain positive.

That kind of playfulness (think of how kids behave when they're learning something new) comes from trusting in a power greater than yourself, i.e., Life Force, to work in the background and nurture your side until it's ready for a full harvest (more on this later).

The third thing you'll do is get into the daily practice of setting the stage. Remember we discussed how each day has a "theme" that seems to play out? The law of deliberate creation works when you set deliberate intentions of how you want your day to go. That doesn't mean you need to detail each and every experience of your day. Instead, identify and intend to feel and be in the specific emotional state you know brings you as close to the highest vibration as possible.

For some people, their highest possible vibration might be hopefulness because for far too long, you've been stuck in themes of fear and disappointment. So, your practical work on a day-to-day basis is training your brain each morning to jump on the hopefulness wagon. You'd set the intention at the start of the day to be and feel hopeful, and to connect with people, experiences, and events that promote a feeling of things working out for you. That's a logical stretch for your brain, and the artist in you would have an easy time imagining things that align with that thought. All you'd have to do is regularly check in (at each hour) to ensure your emotional state is still at that hopeful place, or rising higher. If it drops to pessimism, boredom, or overwhelm, work on getting it back to hopefulness. There are plenty of helpful techniques and meditations you can use in the book's last two chapters.

The bottom line is this: your intentions set the stage for your day and your future manifestation. While we set the big intention to manifest as we list our desires and goals, the real work happens each morning when you train your emotions to set the tone of the day. The more days you can string together where you deliberately and intentionally create more of what you want, the quicker you begin to manifest everything you desire. You must learn to be a deliberate co-creator so the law of attraction can start matching you with more of what you want.

## Your Point of Power

You are your point of power because you transmit signals vibrationally. The most powerful thing you can do, and the job you cannot delegate to anyone or leave to chance, is to remain in the present moment and practice the spiritual law of allowing. It's one thing to learn about the law of attraction, create powerful intentions, and deliberately go into the world expecting good things to come your way. But that doesn't mean you will experience said good. To manifest and experience any desire, we must learn to mentally accept and allow the flow of good. This idea might seem easy, but it trips even the best of us.

At each moment, we're in a constant state of co-creation, though few of us realize it. The present moment is a manifestation of your past dominant thoughts, emotions, intentions, and actions. It's also the starting point for the next thing law of attraction will match you with in the future.

Suppose you're in the common habit of constantly worrying about money. At this moment, you might be entertaining all kinds of negativity and taking minimal inspired action toward financial independence. In that case, your next moments, and the future you'll move into, will be a perfect match of that same instability and concern because the law of attraction cannot match you with prosperity if your dominant signal is still lack.

Conversely, suppose you would use this moment as a kickoff point for deliberate intention to focus on abundance and gratitude. In that case, you'll begin to move into future moments that contain more things that add to that state.

I'm sure you've heard of the famous Biblical phrase, "For whoever has, to him more will be given, and he will have abundance; but whoever does not have, even what he has will be taken away from him." Whether you follow a religious creed or not, the spiritual truth contained in that phrase impacts your daily life. Once you have some momentum from present-moment awareness and allowing the good to come into your life, more will keep showing up. The best time to start creating this positive momentum of abundance is right at this moment. There's a whole chapter dedicated to practices that will enable you to let in more of the good that currently exists in your life, so keep turning the pages and get ready to feel some significant shifts in your world.

***Bonus Tip:*** Pour as much of your energy into the present moment and reach for the highest feeling that sustains it for as long as possible. Give yourself permission to feel good now and find simple things that cause you to experience that feeling of abundance. That's how you quickly build momentum for the greater good.

# Chapter 9

## Visualization and Manifestation

*"When you visualize, then you materialize. If you've been there in the mind, you'll go there in the body."*

— Denis Waitley

D o you know we can only think in pictures? Think about your mom. Now, think about your car, bedroom, fridge, or your favorite restaurant. In all these cases, you didn't see words; you saw images flashing on the screen of your mind. It's a very simple yet profound exercise because it makes you realize that your brain and the process of manifestation require a working image for you to fully believe in the reality of something.

Whenever I speak with someone who claims to understand manifestation, I always ask a simple question: "What is it you desire?" If the person responds with "I want 100K" or "I want to meet my soulmate," I always wonder what image they are holding in their mind as they say those words. The image that flashes in one's mind, combined with the emotional state attached to that image, goes a long way toward securing your manifestation.

Someone once told me they stopped believing in manifesting with the law of attraction because, like Jim Carrey, they wrote themselves a check and carried it everywhere, but they never got the million dollars. Unfortunately, this person wrote the check, but did nothing else to set themselves up for that kind of reality. To claim you want and need 100K while holding an image of "nothingness" is basically shooting yourself in the foot. What the mind cannot perceive and believe, it cannot materialize. That's why we must dedicate enough time to understanding how we form mental pictures and how we can influence the mental images we hold relative to our desires.

Imagination, the secret workshop where all good and bad things are made:

George Bernard Shaw said imagination is the beginning of creation. You imagine what you desire, you will what you imagine, and at last, you create what you will. Imagination has been praised as the key to undreamed future worlds by the best scientific minds and the most prolific mystics. One cannot truly become a law of attraction practitioner and bear witness to the wonders of manifesting until they get a handle on their imagination.

Your imagination is one of five mental faculties that you possess. It is by far the most powerful when it comes to bringing new things into existence. That's how we've been able to advance our society. A few decades ago, no one would have believed we would become a digital economy, that we would buy everything we need from tiny little smartphones and connecting with people across the world through social media platforms. You would have been laughed out of a room if you'd told that story—yet, here we are. Everything we've invented, discovered, and created has come about due to our use of imagination.

In your personal affairs, you must learn to use your imagination creatively. Napoleon Hill wrote in his book that there are two forms of imagination: synthetic and creative imagination.

*Synthetic imagination:* Through this faculty, one may arrange old concepts, ideas, or plans into combinations. This faculty creates nothing, but merely works with the material of experience, education, and observation with which it is fed. It is the faculty used most by the inventor with the exception of the "genius" who draws upon the creative imagination when he cannot solve his problem through synthetic imagination.

*Creative imagination:* Through the faculty of creative imagination, the finite mind of man has direct communication with infinite intelligence. It's the faculty through which "hunches" and "inspirations" are received. It is by this faculty that all basic or new ideas are handed over to man (Hill, *Think and Grow Rich*).

The key to manifesting your greatest desires in life is learning to use and develop your creative imagination. Your creative imagination is the only way to receive insights and action steps that keep you in harmony with what you desire—and ultimately, the surefire way to harmonize your actions with the laws of success. This faculty of the imagination may be developed and exercised into full function no matter how weak it might be currently. The best way to exercise your imagination is to spend regular time visualizing and entertaining the images of your desired outcome.

What is visualization? Simply put, it's the exercise that enables you to activate your imagination in creative ways—that is, playing around with your dreams in a non-material state. You want the ability to see in your mind's eye the reality of your goals so your mind can believe that reality is truc for you. That's why you'll hear many gurus encouraging their followers to spend time daily in their minds, visualizing the thing they want.

Of course, this concept of visualization has been thrown out of proportion and hyperbolized. Considering that we are unique individuals and some of us visualize differently, you may not necessarily find success in posting magazine pictures on a vision board, but that doesn't mean the principle behind this act has failed you; it really is a matter of self-awareness. Figure out how to best tune into your imaginative faculty and play with your visualizing abilities.

Let's take an example of a highly visual woman. She can see things in full color in her mind and tends to catch graphic details others would miss in everyday interactions. When she recounts past memories and events, her ability to recall each detail is mind-blowing and seems effortless to outside observers. Such a woman would have no trouble using visualization techniques to vividly build an image of a future outcome in her mind. As long as she aligns with the rest of the manifesting process, visualization would work incredibly well for her. She would likely preach the power of having a vision board and daily visualizing your desire.

Conversely, let's look at another person—this time, a woman who isn't visual in nature and perceives better through auditory means. This woman's experience of the same visualizing practice wouldn't yield the same results as the first woman simply because their brains are wired differently. This fact is now scientifically proven.

# What Science Has to Say about Visualizing

Adam Zeman, a professor of cognitive and behavioral neurology at the University of Exeter College of Medicine and Health, led a team of researchers to investigate this very topic. They wanted to understand why an estimated 1-3% of people cannot visualize. Zeman termed the inability to visualize "aphantasia" and the ability to visualize "hyperphantasia." To figure out the difference between the two conditions, Zeman and his team conducted their first systematic neuropsychological and brain imaging study for both groups. They performed functional magnetic resonance imaging (fMRI) scans on 24 participants with aphantasia, 25 with hyperphantasia, and 20 people with mid-range imagery vividness who were part of a control group. In addition to these scans, they also evaluated detailed cognitive and personality tests.

Researchers observed that hyperphantasics had a stronger connection between the parts of the brain related to vision and frontal regions connected to decision-making and attention. The results? All groups displayed similar scores on standard memory tests; however, people with hyperphantasia gave richer descriptions of imagined scenarios than the control group. They had a stronger ability to remember events in their lives. Aphantastics couldn't access that level of detail and struggled to recognize faces as well as the hyperphantasics. Adam Zeman concluded that "there are big, invisible differences between us in the ability to visualize, and these are linked to the differences in the ways our brain work" (Cassata, 2021).

## Importance of Regular Visualization

- **Building momentum -** Visualizing your dream causes you to focus your attention on what you want. Where attention goes, energy flows, enabling you to build momentum toward full manifestation.
- **Increase your confidence -** The more you visualize yourself in the reality of your dream, the more trust you'll generate within yourself. Over time, this trust increases your sense of self-worth as you start to believe that you deserve to have this as your new norm.

- ***Uncover your resistance -*** As you visualize, you will become aware of the areas where frustration, stress, and anxiety creep in. This awareness will enable you to know which limiting beliefs and negative emotions to work on so your visualization can be more enjoyable. As the exercise becomes more enjoyable, it will be easy to activate the right emotions that will signal what you really want to the universe.

- ***Motivating and strengthening discipline -*** Many people find visualization helps them feel motivated and excited to get up in the morning and work hard for their dream. It's a great reminder of what you're working for and moving toward.

## Visualizing Exercise

Let's do a little litmus test to see how visually inclined you are. Close your eyes for a moment and think of a red rose. Can you see the petals, the richness of the red? How detailed is that rose, and do you see it standing in a vase or as part of a rose bush?

How clear is that imagery to you? Or, do you see nothing at all?

The above research published in the journal *Cerebral Cortex Communications* helps us recognize why we may or may not be good at visualizing. If we realize we fall into the mid-range visualizers or perhaps even the aphantasia group, all hope isn't lost. Just because visualization is not our superpower doesn't mean we can't strengthen it as one would strengthen their muscles through regular exercise. It does, however, require enough self-awareness to encourage ourselves to lean into the other ways we can easily perceive, create, and even imagine things. For example, I am better at creating and perceiving new images through sound and smell. So, in this rose exercise, I would focus more on smelling it and listening for environmental sounds to determine whether I am visualizing my rose in the middle of a garden with birds chirping or in a kitchen table vase. There's no wrong or right way to visualize as long as it's the right way for your brain. Always remember that.

# How Specific Should I Get?

Remember our earlier clarification about the law of attraction, how it's not a tool or something you can use or manipulate into giving you what you want? Well, that need to control or "use" a tool that will get you what you desire can now be drawn upon because visualization is precisely that—a tool that you can use and manipulate. But to what end?

For the sole purpose of bringing your thoughts, feelings, and imagination into harmony. When you can see images that put you into the feeling and thinking state of having your manifestation, you've won.

So, suppose you're wondering how to do visualization right or how specific you should get. In that case, the short and proper answer is this: be as specific as your "feelings" allow you to be.

What matters is that you can genuinely feel you are the person living in that desired reality. You should act like and feel that it's already done. So ask yourself, what kind of imagery do I craft in my imagination to enable me to act like, feel, and believe I am already in possession of my dream? That's what visualization is all about.

If you spend time daily visualizing your dream, but it doesn't "feel good" and you come away from that exercise feeling impatient, frustrated, hopeless, or doubtful, the desired manifestation will not show up.

## How Long Should I Visualize?

As long as you need to cultivate the high-frequency feeling and certainty of your dream. For some people, that's a minute; for others, it's five minutes, and for others still, it takes twenty minutes at least to hit that sweet spot. Time should not be a factor when it comes to connecting with the reality of your dream. Instead, you must focus on how you feel and what you perceive.

## Does Visualization Help Manifesting Happen Faster?

The jury is out on this question because like I said, visualizing is a powerful tool for those possessing the ability to vividly see things, and sometimes a handicap for those who feel utterly blind in their mind. Regardless of how clearly you see things in your mind, the law of attraction works, and manifestations are coming your way. The time it takes for you to match up with your dream is more about releasing the resistance and disbelief that often distorts your vibrational alignment. Many of the key ingredients that determine how quickly manifestation occurs are discussed in the subsequent chapters. And while visualizing doesn't create a manifesting shortcut for you, it does help you build momentum and positive expectations. That is, as you put your attention on the reality of what you want, energy flows in that direction and the law of attraction responds accordingly.

Visualization is excellent for uncovering resistance and limiting beliefs:

One of the main reasons I like to encourage people to engage in active visualization is that it makes you aware of the work you need to do to get into that believing state. For example, if your desire is to start your business and earn an annual income of seven figures, and as you visualize and struggle to see any signs of success, then you know that struggle is something to work on. That is, there are doubts active in you that don't align with your desire. Perhaps it's low self-worth or fear of failure, but whatever it is, the fact that you can't sit for a few minutes and use your imagination to connect with that good feeling-state of being a successful entrepreneur tells you something is off. You might be saying you dream of being an entrepreneur, but your vibrational offering is that you can't.

Abraham Hicks said and even wrote a book called *Ask, and It Is Given*. That's the simple manifesting process, and it is valid for the most part. But when you have plenty of resistance to what you've asked for, there's some in-between work you'll have to do before it can be given to you. If you'd like to know how much resistance you have concerning your dream, start visualizing and noting the emotional tone and the thoughts that linger around the dream. Notice what's coming up and the aspects that don't feel good to you as you envision. Are there beliefs coming up, or past memories? Even if it seems random to you, trust that you're receiving insights that shouldn't be ignored.

When you first start visualizing your dream, it won't be smooth, and that's okay. Don't try to fix anything; simply observe and witness the chaos like a journalist. Let the entire scenario play out to completion without judgment. For example, you might desire to marry your soulmate as my friend did. When I introduced him to this process, he reported that whenever he sat down to visualize, he would see himself speaking with a beautiful girl, but then she would say she was not interested and walk away. In fact, he started having dreams of her turning him down over and over again. Those dreams were very disheartening for my friend, but I told him this was great news—it meant his mind was pointing out the resistance he needed to fix before the law of attraction could finally work in his favor. His long history of heartache and abuse from his mother was still active in him, and it needed to be resolved before his mind could finally accept and believe in true love and a healthy relationship.

When my friend finally manifested the love of his life, it wasn't because he was spending time visualizing in great detail his relationship. In fact, he was very general in his visualization and opted to focus more on feeling a certain way. That feeling is the same one he has today after five years of marriage to his soulmate.

# Why Visualizing Your Goals May Not Be Working and What To Do about It

Perhaps you're reading this and thinking, "I've been trying to visualize my goal, but nothing happens!" You likely didn't follow the rules of creative visualization. As you've learned in this chapter, proper visualization involves:

- Employing your imagination.
- Intentionally summoning the desired emotion.
- Engaging the right senses to aid you in that visualizing process.

It's important to pause at this point and figure out where things fell apart in your process. Remember, the universal laws are always at work, and you are constantly vibrating something to the universe. So if your manifesting is delayed or absent, the error that must be corrected lies in your thinking and actions. Sometimes, the error is as simple as not having clarity about what you truly desire. At other times, it's that what you want isn't really a burning desire and lacks the proper "juice," so to speak, to keep you persistently going for it until it materializes. It could also be that you're still entertaining negative self-talk, or worse still, you doubt whether you can really accomplish your desire.

People often confess that when they get brutally honest about their creative visualization, they become aware that lingering in the back of their mind is the thought, "How can my imagination possibly change events in the physical world?" This doubtful thought can poison any seeds you've planted in your imagination and hinder mani-festation.

Perhaps the biggest culprit when it comes to the success or failure of this technique is a lack of self-awareness. You must learn to pick and choose processes and practices that align with your person-ality and feel most believable to you. What do I mean by this?

Todd discovered the creative visualization technique back when he was a freshman. But no matter what he tried or how hard he visualized the kind of life he desired, nothing changed. By the time he graduated in clinical psychology, he'd gathered enough research that finally enabled him to uncover where he'd gone wrong all these years. He realized that his way of creative visualization (following what gurus had told him) was ineffective. Upon reflection, he admitted to himself that he'd never really bought the idea of just sitting in bed in the morning and seeing that million-dollar check or getting that "A" in his final exam. Yet, that's precisely what Todd had been doing. But instead of falling into despair and quitting, Todd intuitively felt he should tweak his creative visualization into something "more believable" for him.

All the books he'd read described visualizing the finished product. He struggled to believe in that finished product, so instead, he chose a scenario that caused him to feel like he was well on the way to getting the final outcome, but he focused more on a particular "action" that caused him to feel good, deserving, and finally ready for that final manifestation. This modification in his creative visualization proved to be the key that unlocked his manifesting powers. Today, Todd believes this method is the best way to visualize your desire. It certainly worked for him, so does that mean you should also do the same?

Maybe. The truth is, there is no right or wrong way. The only thing that matters is that you visualize your desire in the manner that feels most real to you and evokes the highest frequency (emotionally speaking).

As long as it feels "fake" or "wishful," it's not right for you.

The solution to ineffective visualization, especially if you've done it for several months or years to no avail, is to get candid with yourself. What is your personality? Are you more of a doer? Do you tend to enjoy the "process" of any activity, or the outcome? The more self-aware you are about what makes you tick, the easier it will be to customize your creative visualization experience for maximum benefit. For some who read this book, their best creative visualization exercise is to pick an event that would occur after the manifestation takes place, e.g., driving their new car, sitting in their new corner office, receiving that million-dollar check, etc. For others, their best use of creative visualization is to pick a scenario at that point in their life where they take an action they know and believe will lead them toward the manifestation. In fact, athletes use this method all the time; they tend to visualize doing jump shots and mentally rehearse their actions rather than holding up the trophy or the after-party once they win the championship.

See where this is going? Suppose you're more of a doer personality. In that case, you're likely to experience more success visualizing actions that make you feel good and confident about the reality of your desire, whatever that might be. So, practice and mentally rehearse that scene repeatedly until you feel it's done.

# Visualization Hacks and Techniques That Work for Anyone

Whether you're strong in visualizing or not, here are some proven techniques that will enable you to generate the feeling-state necessary for your manifestation. Remember, details don't matter, so if you tend to get attached and create resistance when you get detailed in your visualization, stick to generalized visualizations.

### #1: Remember That Time When You Felt the Same Way

**Suitable for:** Highly visual people and those who aren't.

As the name of this technique suggests, this visualization exercise is excellent for everyone. Whether you're skilled at seeing vividly in your mind's eye or not, all you need to do is emphasize and focus on the emotion. Here's how to carry out this practice:

Get into a relaxed state, take deep soothing breaths, and close your eyes if it helps. Ask yourself, "What emotion do I want to stir up that matches my dream?" Now, think of a time in the past when you experienced the same feelings. For example, suppose the feeling you'll have once your dream manifests is that of joy, relaxation, and abundance. In that case, you might envision a time when you were on a memorable vacation that made you feel all those things. Keep your eyes closed and recall that experiencc to mind. What do you remember most? Soak yourself in that imagery until your feelings stabilize, then do your best to carry that emotional state with you into the rest of your day.

I like to use this particular practice a lot. A memorable experience that's travel-related is a memory of lying on the white sandy beaches in Zanzibar sipping a margarita while the sun was setting. Whenever I drift into that scenario, I can smell the warm air infused with the saltiness of the ocean. I can recall the breeze against my skin and the relaxing sounds of the waves. This memory gets me in that feeling of abundance and relaxation instantly!

## #2: Pink Bubble Technique

**Suitable for:** Mid-range to highly visual people

This technique comes from Shakti Gawain's book *Creative Visualization: Use the Power of Imagination to Create What You Want in Life.* Here's how to do it:

Imagine your dream has already manifested in full. Picture it as clearly as you can in your mind's eye. Now, imagine a pink bubble (like the bubbles kids blow at parties or something balloon-like) and place that representation of your dream inside the pink bubble. Allow it to float up and away into the sky. As the pink bubble floats away, consciously let it go, knowing that it is already done. Doing this is symbolic of you detaching from that outcome and intentionally releasing any tension, stress, or worry about its reality. This action signals to the universe that you know it's real and trust that the universe must deliver in due time.

**Pro tip:** The key here is to access that certainty that your dream is absolute and fully connect with that emotional certainty before placing it into the pink bubble. Then once you do, never go back to questioning its reality as that will undo your intention.

## #3: Enter the Picture

**Suitable for:** People who are mid-range to highly visual.

This exercise will involve a lot of imagination and vivid imagery. The more you can see graphic details for this exercise, the better. It's also meant to be a lot of fun, so if you find yourself getting frustrated or struggling to engage with higher-frequency emotions, then consider choosing a different practice. It also demands that you learn to become proactive in your movie-making. Here's how to do it.

First, you need to determine with great clarity what you really desire and set a definite game plan for attaining it. Let's assume your dream is to get promoted to regional VP at your company and you think it will take you two years to get there. Great.

The next thing you need to do is close your eyes and imagine you're about two years down the line in your life. Looking at this future, you'll be pretty much the same in terms of appearance, but you've had your new VP title for a few months.

Now, look back through your phone at some pictures of a significant event related to your goal. Let's say, photos of your night out to celebrate your big promotion. Actively scroll through your phone and notice the images you took to remember that moment and feel good about the event. As you continue to go through the pictures in your imagination, you come across an image that stands out. So, you enlarge the photo and imagine you're "entering" that photo. Inside the picture at that location, everything has come to life, and you are now experiencing everything that took place that day. Look around you, explore, see, hear, touch, smell, and taste the experiences surrounding your achievement of this goal. What were you wearing? Where were you? Was it a dinner where your best friend made a champagne toast in your honor and said some nice things? What did he say? Who else is there with you? What foods were served?

Get as detailed and visceral as you can without frustrating yourself. The most important thing is having fun and enjoying visualizing your future success.

**Pro tip:** Stick to a single scene and play it repeatedly until it feels authentic.

## #4: Vision Board

**Suitable for:** Everyone who is predominantly a visual or kinesthetic learner

I'm sure you've heard of vision boards and probably watched videos from Jack Canfield and John Assaraf or even the movie *The Secret.* They all claim having a vision board is an excellent secret for manifesting. And while it's not really a secret ingredient, it does help, especially if you're the kind of person who needs something physical to look at during the manifesting process. Here's how to do it:

As long as you're creative, you can develop any kind of vision board (virtual or physical) that enables you to feel connected to your dream. The idea behind a vision board is to create something that helps you physically identify your goals, whether they are spiritual, romantic, financial, or something else. Vision boards can be made out of inexpensive materials. You can use magazine cut-outs, photos, or other images to create your collage, mapping out the future you're building at this moment. Hang the vision board where you can see it daily. Sit and look at your vision board as regularly as possible to put yourself in that reality of your manifested dream mentally and emotionally.

# Chapter 10

## *Creating the Right States for Manifesting Your Desires*

*"Whatever we plant in our subconscious mind and nourish with repetition and emotion will one day become a reality."*

— Earl Nightingale

ack in chapter 1, we introduced the law of vibration. You learned that manifesting isn't about trying to control the law of attraction; instead, it's about learning to manage your vibrational offering, or the energy you put out into the universe. Why? Because the law of vibration is the primary law that determines the workings of the law of attraction. Hence, it follows that the more in control you are of your vibrations (given that you're a vibrational being), the easier it will be to predict your outcomes.

Furthermore, the law of attraction can only match you with corresponding experiences. But how does one control their vibration?

The easiest and best way to successfully control your vibrational offerings is to control your emotions. Emotions are often misunderstood. Most humans still have a lot to learn about the role and power of emotions. Although thoughts are essential, controlling what you think is a futile task as the average human being processes between 60,000-70,000 thoughts each day. Trying to manage that amount means you'll never get anything else done. Besides, your brain would probably quit after the first hour. Therefore, a better strategy is to control your emotions.

What you feel represents a vibrational state that your brain interprets as an emotion. That vibrational state is a culmination of your focus, beliefs, thinking patterns, physiology, level of awareness, and more. If your vibrational state is low and dense, you'll experience it as a low or negative emotional state. Conversely, if you're experiencing a positive emotional state, you're transmitting very high and fast vibrational frequency. The trick and primary job of manifesting your dream life is to stabilize and normalize those high vibrational frequencies and operate from there most of the time.

You manifest what you are vibrationally—not what you want.

If you desire more money and say you want more money, but your vibrational state is hopelessness, anxiety, and worry, you won't manifest more. The same is true if you desire to manifest a romantic relationship, better health, a promotion, or anything else you can think of. Think of your vibrational frequency as a point of attraction. Since you initiate and offer that point of attraction, it is accurate to say that universal laws can never fail to deliver what you request.

Martha was in her thirties and anxious that she had never been married and her clock was ticking. Her lifelong dream was to get married and have three or four children, yet she was not close to materializing that desire. When she first came across the law of attraction, she was excited and thought, "Finally, I can have my dream life."

Many books and seminars later, she was still miserable and single. During a weekend seminar, she learned from her teacher that manifesting was about making yourself an attraction magnet. In her lack of awareness, she thought, "I just need to put in more effort in attracting the right guy." So, Martha put in a lot of effort to meet her future husband. She asked everyone she knew to introduce her to a single guy, joined online dating sites, and started attending networking events and meet-ups, assuming these actions were how to meet Mr. Right. Another six months went by, and one day, after many failed dates from her online dating sites, she seemed to have landed a guy. A few weeks later, they planned to meet in person. Martha was convinced he was the one.

Unfortunately, he was far from Mr. Right. Everything about their relationship felt forced. She couldn't bring herself to admit it because her ego was too consumed by the need to have a man in her life. When she joined our support group, it was out of sheer despair because of how unhappy she was in her relationship. Things were out of hand, and she missed the time when she was excited about the prospect of a family. Now she felt trapped in a relationship she could see had no future.

Martha's story isn't uncommon. We see many variations of this outcome play out in people's lives when action is forced. That doesn't mean the dream was wrong or the universe became capricious; instead, it's an indicator that somewhere in the process of manifesting, we violated the laws of success. Our point of attraction didn't match up with what we wanted, so in an attempt to "force" things into being, we took steps that brought us what we don't like!

Going back to Martha's story, consider for a moment what her vibrational offering must have been as she forced herself to join clubs and ask for blind dates. Do you suppose she was in a high emotional state, or a low desperate state with a keen awareness of lacking a man in her life? That is no way to attract your ideal partner because again, what you are is what you match up with. If only Martha had learned beforehand that her main job was to establish and maintain the right state of being first, then whatever inspired action she'd have taken would have resulted in more pleasing results. Her point of attraction would have been ideal.

To match up with your ideal, establish the right vibrational point of attraction:

Many law of attraction students feels discouraged when they read this chapter because to them, it's impossible to see the reality of something you've never had. If that's a concern you have, here's the simple antidote: don't worry about seeing something if you've never had it. Instead, place all your attention on the highest vibrational frequency you have access to now, and build upon that.

If you're dirt-poor and all you've ever known is abject poverty, trying to see, think, and feel rich will be in vain. Attempting to see a million dollars in your mind is going to feel impossible. And even if you do see it for an instant, you won't sustain that thought for very long. Soon enough, your poverty thoughts will flood back in. So, how would you possibly climb out of that pit of poverty? By changing your state of being and starting right where you are with what you've already got.

# Change Your State, and You Will Change Your Life

Every experience you have and every reality you've known are mere states of being. Sickness is a state of being, and so is health. Poverty is a state of being, and so is prosperity. To begin changing your state of being, you must make a deliberate decision to move your emotions higher up that emotional scale we discussed earlier. The higher you go, the higher your frequency rises, and so does your point of attraction. There are two things you can leverage to change your emotions anytime, anywhere, and these things are your attention and your body.

To change your attention, shift your focus. Where do you choose to place your attention throughout the day? Is your mind trained to look for destructive and negative things, or have you taught it to look for the good? For millions of years, our brains were more focused on survival, which meant they were constantly scanning for threats. Being aware of all the negative around us helped us stay alive. Still, this same ability has become a source of anguish in today's society. It causes us to misuse our power and dwell on destructive things.

159

To change your body, you need to become more self-aware and take note of your posture, your body's energy levels, and alertness. If your body is neglected, it's unlikely to feel sharp, energetic, and healthy. A body that doesn't feel healthy will have poor focus and, in turn, lower emotions, both of which impact your point of attraction. That's why proper sleep, good nutrition, exercise, and keeping good posture are always advised.

Realize that everything is connected. There's an unbreakable body-mind-spirit connection that you need to become aware of. The more you honor and maintain harmony in all three domains of your existence, the easier it will be to establish and sustain higher frequency emotions. These higher frequency emotions will ultimately raise your point of attraction to allow the law of attraction to match you with every good thing on your path.

## Tips to Effectively Change Your State for Abundance and Prosperity

The foundational state of being that every powerful manifester needs to master is the state of gratitude.

Gratitude is, in fact, something we all have access to because no matter where we are or how bad things appear, we can always find something to feel grateful for. Even the poorest among us can gain access to this state with just a little deliberate effort and powerful intentions. And when you can access gratitude, you can access prosperity.

So, if you're wondering where to begin or which state to reach for as often as possible, start with gratitude. We'll discuss ways of cultivating this state in a later chapter. For now, let's talk about simple techniques you can use to change your emotions and, ultimately, your mental state.

## #1: Smile More

Yes, it sounds so simple, but I promise you, if you've been carrying through life feeling worried, anxious, and grumpy, this will be a tough one. Most adults feel so gloomy and sour, they don't even realize how rare it is for them to wear a smile for an hour, let alone for a day. There's no shortage of things that can put a smile on your face, and with a bit of effort, that smile will become consistent, and so will your improved emotions.

A smile can be mighty because it sends positive signals to your brain. It can even trick your brain into thinking you're feeling better than you actually are, and that's all you need to start shifting vibrationally. Your mind doesn't know what's real or "made up"; it only reads the signals offered. So if you look yourself in the mirror, say something nice about yourself and feel good, that's enough to shift your current vibration. Sometimes, looking in the mirror isn't enough to keep that smile on all day, so find other ways of compensating, like putting on your favorite playlist while driving, watching a funny video during your work breaks, watching some comedy in the evening, or looking at old pictures that warm your heart just before bedtime.

## #2: Increase Your Positive Self-talk

There's an inner dialogue that's ever taking place throughout the day. Some call it the "inner critic" because of how negative this voice tends to be. As you read this book, that dialogue is taking place, and you're either carrying on an argument with me in your mind or agreeing with these ideas. It's important to know the dominant tone of your inner dialogue. Only then can you make the connection between how you usually feel and what the law of attraction matches you up with. If you typically feel anxious, overwhelmed, frustrated, doubtful, stressed, unhappy, inadequate, or lacking, much of that is rooted in your ongoing "story" and inner self-talk.

Suppose you have an inner critic that constantly reminds you that you're poor, not smart enough, not good enough, etc. In that case, it's tough to vibrate at the higher frequencies that attract prosperity. To improve your self-talk, get more curious and question all your negative thoughts. The harsh tone and words may feel true, but are they really? Experts on this subject matter recommend that anytime we catch a negative conversation, we should stop and ask ourselves how much of that information is true and factual. Most of the time, our tortuous thoughts fall short of being both true and accurate.

So, just because you have a thought doesn't mean you should accept it. Consider using the simple "yes, but..." technique. For example, let's say your inner voice says, "Don't share your idea with your colleagues. They'll just laugh at you." In response to that inner critic, you could say, "Yes, but what if they don't?" See how simple this shift can be? It will take time, practice, and a lot of patience, so I suggest trying this new positive talk in one area of your life first. Choose the area where you tend to be hardest on yourself. Think about how you would prefer to feel about that area and come up with positive statements that are intentional. Please don't force it or exaggerate; reach for words that feel realistic and acceptable enough to your mind. Even if it's not the most positive thought, if it feels better than what you've currently been saying about yourself, that's the right step. Now keep reinforcing it and building momentum until you can tell the most positive things about yourself without creating a sense of "fakeness."

## #3: Recognize the Power of Your Thoughts

Are you aware of the dominant thought patterns that run your life? Spend a few moments now observing the type of thoughts circulating in your head without judgment. Do this regularly over the next 21 days and record it so you can start to see patterns emerging at the end of the experiment. Then, you'll see the correlation between your thinking and circumstances in life.

Pick an area of your life where results are less than pleasing and ask yourself, "Are my thoughts in this domain of my life rooted in abundance or lack?" Be open, honest, and non-judgmental. Once you get an answer, ask again, "What can I do today to shift to a more abundant mindset?" Write down at least one simple step that you can take within the next 24 hours and commit to doing it. The more you can show yourself that you can shift your thought patterns, the easier it will be to maintain the right state.

## #4: Notice the Good

Most of the time, you'll shift into a negative state because something triggers you. Instead of falling into that pit of despair and messing with your alignment, choose to step back and take a more holistic perspective. Taking this action will instantly stabilize your state of being. Rather than focusing on what's going wrong or the negativity that's putting you down, find something that's going right as it relates to that subject matter. For example, the fact that you've realized your state has changed into negative means your emotional guidance system is working perfectly. At least you have control over that system, and you can at least work on your energy and uplift yourself even as you attempt to brainstorm and resolve the current challenge. See how simple it can be to refocus and gain a new perspective?

## #5: Use Positive Affirmations That Move You to a Higher Frequency

Compelling evidence from Carnegie Mellon University shows that positive affirmations can decrease signs of stress and improve problem-solving skills. This is fantastic news for us because it implies we can change our state at will just by identifying, memorizing, and recalling the right statements of truth that raise our vibration. The trick here is to personalize and design a list of affirmative statements that engage your logic and emotions in an instant.

Below, I've share a list of affirmative statements that work for me. Feel free to copy and modify them to suit your personality or, better still, use them for inspiration as you come up with your own unique creations. Keep in mind that speaking positive statements to yourself might feel awkward at first, but it will become natural with enough practice, and the impact will be instantaneous. Even superheroes know the value of using affirmations to change their state—just watch *Antman* and note how often Scott

Lang, aka Antman, uses positive affirmations to keep himself encouraged.

- I believe in myself.
- I choose to embrace the mysteries of life.
- I am my best source of motivation.
- I am capable of achieving greatness.
- I am a powerful creator and I create the life I want on my terms.
- I am always open-minded and eager to explore new avenues to success.
- I stay focused on my vision and passionately pursue my daily work.
- I choose positivity.
- I am enough.
- I am growing and changing for the better.
- Today is a great day to be alive.
- I am strong, powerful, and can face anything.
- I face challenging situations with confidence, courage, and conviction.
- All my problems have solutions.
- I am getting better at the game of life every day.
- I conquer every obstacle to create my dream life.

- I let go of negativity and find the good in this moment.
- All my experiences are essential for my growth and development.
- Nobody but me decides how I feel.
- I am in charge and in control of my thoughts and emotions.

# Chapter 11

## *Love, Faith, and the Law of Attraction*

*"The Universe likes speed. Don't delay. Don't second-guess. Don't doubt. When the opportunity is there, when the impulse is there, when the intuitive nudge from within is there, act. That's your job. And that's all you have to do."*

— Dr. Joe Vitale

I'm glad you're still here because you've finally started awakening to the simple truths that will have the most significant impact on your life. Many people don't realize that manifesting one's dream life isn't so much about managing the law of attraction as it is about managing one's emotions and point of attraction. And that is: if you're not driven by love, your manifestations will always fall short.

This chapter will be short and sweet, focused on opening your eyes to this one idea.

## The Two Driving Forces in Life

In the Native American tradition, we find the tale of the two wolves. The story is about two characters—a grandfather and his grandson. The grandfather says, "I have a fight going on in me. It's taking place between two wolves. One is evil—he is anger, envy, sorrow, regret, greed, arrogance, self-pity, guilt, resentment, inferiority, lies, false pride, superiority, and ego." The grandfather paused for a moment, looked at the grandson, and then went on,

"The other wolf embodies all my positive emotions. He is peace, hope, joy, serenity, humility, kindness, generosity, truth, compassion, and faith. Both wolves are fighting to the death. That same fight is going on inside you and every other person."

The grandson took a moment to reflect on this. After several moments of silence, he looked up at his grandfather and asked innocently, "Which will win?"

The old man's responded in a calm, reassuring voice. "The one you feed."

This story is one of my favorite parables because it carries deep meaning for the awakened soul. The origin of this story remains unknown, but historians typically attribute the tale to the Cherokee or the Lenape people. Regardless of where it came from, you and I can learn a lot from understanding what the grandfather taught his grandson. Think of the two wolves as fear and love in the context of this book. The "evil wolf" is fear, and all destructive emotions come under that banner. On the other hand, the "good wolf" is love, where all positive and constructive emotions reside. If we feed fear and live from this driving force, all our efforts at evoking the laws of success to bring forth our dream lifestyle will be in vain; evil always destroys our good efforts. Even if we can temporarily manifest some success by sheer force and relentless willpower, the poison from the evil wolf will quickly kill our hard work.

Remember how we said energy is everything? Fear has a distinct vibrational frequency. The energy one radiates while in a state of fear opposes that which another radiates when in a state of love. I have learned that if I can regularly check in with myself to ensure that I am living life from a place of love and I've chosen my goals out of love, then by default, my manifestation will always be pleasing.

# What Drives You? What Influences Your Desires?

These two questions should always be at the forefront of your mind. If you're wondering how to tell which driving force is acting strongly in your life, look at the following list.

When driven by fear, people will:

- Express and create doubt.
- Hold grudges and petty grievances.
- Make excuses and try to cover up mistakes.
- Sugarcoat the truth.
- Hold on to resentment and seek revenge.
- Act passive-aggressively and avoid confrontation at all costs.
- Run away from the possibility of failure and avoid taking any risks.

When driven by love, people will:

- Build confidence in themselves and those around them.
- Choose their desires based on what they love and want more of.
- Admit their mistakes and do what's necessary to correct and learn from mistakes.
- Run toward the possibility of success.
- Easily forgive and forget.
- Boldly take action and calculated risks as they go after their dreams.
- Express kindness, compassion, and the courage to have tough or hard candid conversations.

## How to Practice Being Driven by the Force of Love

In the beginning, and for most of your life, faith is what enables you to dream and manifest the best in life. And when you can focus on feeding the good wolf, you are guaranteed to have both faith and love because the two are inseparable—just like fear and doubt are also inseparable.

A good rule of thumb to help you figure out which wolf is more dominant within you is to identify how much faith (or lack thereof) you're operating with. As you think about your chosen desire or your dream life, do you experience 100% faith? If not, how much doubt is present? Anytime you struggle to feel faith, the evil wolf is strangling the good wolf, and your immediate action should be to get yourself in a state of love.

If you take nothing else from this book, let it be this: without love and faith, your manifestation will continue to be a struggle. The real work isn't to believe in the law of attraction; instead, it's about having faith, moving through the world from a consciousness of love, and feeding the good wolf all day long until eventually, the evil wolf grows weak and incapable of poisoning your vibration.

# Chapter 12

## *The Art of Allowing*

*"Ask for what you want and be prepared to get it."*

— Maya Angelou

Allowing is a complicated art we must learn if we want the law of attraction to continue working for us for all our lives. It's good that we've reached the point where our desire is clearly outlined, our intention is firm, and we're taking charge of our emotions. We now understand the importance of engaging the imagination and raising our vibrations through high-frequency thoughts and feelings. We've also learned the importance of switching from fear to love on this journey.

The next step in mastering the creative process is subtle and often overlooked. Most of us don't realize how necessary it is to deliberately allow the good we desire. Our society only emphasizes hard work, persistence, and maximum effort in achieving a goal; these attributes are all good and needed along the journey. Still, they do us no good if we compromise our emotional state or if we're not openly allowing that good we're working hard to materialize.

When I start talking about relaxing into a state of allowing your good to come in, people assume I disregard the role of action and hard work in our lives. That couldn't be further from the truth. The law of attraction isn't about sitting on your bed meditating all day long, waiting for money to fall into your lap. It's also not about living recklessly. Equally true is that success doesn't mean working yourself to exhaustion and suffering burnout as a result. Overworking oneself is just as detrimental to one's prosperity in life as are lethargy and idleness. In both extreme cases, allowing isn't taking place, and the laws of success are violated.

# So What Is Allowing?

Allowing is about saying yes to your good. It's about allowing EVERYTHING to be okay with you just as it is or, in other words, making peace with other people, situations, and life itself. It is accepting that life has your back even if it doesn't seem that way and learning to detach from the thing you desire so it doesn't turn you into an enslaved person.

Another critical aspect of allowing is creating room for the good you wish to come in. In the next chapter, we'll talk about this latter aspect and how you can make room for prosperity in your life. For now, let's turn our focus to the former aspect of allowing, which can be pretty hard to wrap our minds around. Saying yes to your good and trusting it's already yours when you can't physically see it can at first feel impossible. Your senses and ego struggle to believe that your manifestation will come to you if you're not exerting physical effort.

To some extent, that feeling of "I need to make it happen" is good because action on your end is required; however, action should never be forced. If you're drowning in doubt and frustration, no amount of hard work will bring about full manifestation. The opposite of allowing is resisting, and *gosh*, are we masters at creating resistance to the good we desire. If you've had a desire for a long time and still don't see it manifesting, you've got resistance keeping you from allowing and manifesting the desire.

I know what you're thinking. "How can I ever do something to keep me apart from my desire?" Well, it's not intentional, but given the experience of delay and absence of desire, it's definitely happening.

## How Resistance Can Block Manifestation

Remember the story of the woman who forcefully tried to manifest Mr. Right only to end up in a relationship she didn't want? That's a clear example of how we can set up resistance around our desire and block the positive manifestation. Her actions to find a soulmate were rooted in fear and lack. Instead of allowing love into her life, she forced things to happen, which only amplified her sense of lack. Her fear that time was running out and her biological clock was ticking only caused her to feed the "evil wolf" even more. That meant she unconsciously played with images of loneliness, failure, etc. She might have been feeling jealous of others who seemed happily married, and all her anxious thoughts probably crowded her judgment and choices as she went on dates. I can imagine how strong this negative vibration grew as she recounted how awful and unfruitful her dating life was to friends and family. All these actions buried her deeper into her problem instead of paving the way for love. That's the resistance we're referring to.

So the trick is to clean up your resistance and allow your good. Say yes in a way that increases your certainty. Take inspired action, walk in faith, and live in the expectation that you're moving one step closer to your reality with every step and choice.

It's easier said than done, I know. So let's talk about ways you can practice the art of allowing immediately.

# Tips for Allowing

## #1: Building a Bridge

It's essential to clean up your resistance before you practice allowing it. That doesn't mean you just slap yourself some positive affirmations as these will do very little to stabilize the right vibrations when you're knee-deep in resistance.

First, we need to slow down the momentum of that resistance, and the best way to do so to practice what I call bridge thoughts. Through bridge thoughts, you can lift yourself out of the negative side of manifestation and build positive momentum where affirmations become valid.

Suppose you've been looking to manifest a desire for a long time with no success. In that case, this will require patience, compassion, and time because those limiting beliefs won't deactivate permanently at the snap of a finger; however, you can start where you are to think and feel different. So, suppose your desire is financial abundance and you desire to earn income you've never made. In that case, the bridge thought to clean up resistance should be more generic, e.g., "I know this universe is abundant. I can see it all around me. I am abundant in some areas of my life already, and I realize that abundance is my birthright."

So, give your attention to abundance in general instead of focusing on the specific desire. Remember, life is intelligence, and it already knows what you desire. Even if you're not focusing on that particular amount of money, as you get into the flow of abundance and stabilize it, the law of attraction will match you with all your desires, including cash. Once you've stabilized yourself in abundance and feel like a vibrational match to the good you want, it's time to practice allowing.

## #2: Let Go and Detach

This part is pretty hard for our egos, yet it's the best way to practice allowing. Deepak Chopra teaches it as one of the spiritual laws of success, and he calls it detachment. Letting go and detaching from our desire is actually allowing it to manifest. Sounds counterintuitive, I know, but just suspend your disbelief for a moment and hear me out.

No one suggests you let go of the desire or your intention to have it. Instead, you're encouraged to give up your attachment to the how and when. Living in a non-attached way to the outcome of what you intend to experience liberates you and raises your vibration. Why? Because spiritual detachment can't be faked, and it can only come from a place of "knowing." That level of trust in life frees you from the need to control anything. So, as your ego gives up control, divine intelligence takes over and the laws naturally do their thing.

Ancient wisdom traditions have always taught that stepping into the unknown while surrendering ourselves and our desires to the divine mind is the best way to experience all the good life offers. It takes a special kind of mindset—one that's abundant and filled with faith and creative flow—to step into the unknown, and that's the work you need to do to prime your mind and develop such a mindset.

**Pro tip:** Bring to mind a goal or desire you've longed for. Practice detaching by staying grounded in the wisdom of uncertainty while positively expecting a solution. If you're genuinely unattached, you won't feel compelled to force things into place. Instead, you'll be mindful, alert, and on the lookout for synchronistic opportunities. Prepare yourself in every possible way to meet your goals and intentionally pursue the activities that amplify your joy as you go about your life, then make room for that good to come in.

### #3: Appreciate

Get into the habit of praising and appreciating the good you currently perceive. When you wake up in the morning, praise this new day and the gift of life that is yours. Find the little things that are working in your life, such as the fact that you have an abundance of hot water to shower in or a comfortable bed at night. If you're walking past a garden or park, note how abundant the trees, leaves, and flowers appear. All that is abundance, and you are part of that flow of abundance as well. Immerse yourself as much as possible in nature, where it's easy to find things to marvel at, praise, and appreciate as you build this habit of allowing and perceiving good in your life.

Over time, and with a lot of practice, this noticing of abundance will turn into a habit and, ultimately, a mindset (an abundant mindset). That's when people will start asking you, "What's your secret? How is it that you always get what you want?"

# Chapter 13

## *Sending the Right Signals to the Universe*

*"Like attracts like. You have to understand: you are a magnet. Whatever you are, that's what you draw to you. If you're negative, you're going to draw negativity. You positive? You draw positive. You're a kind person? Most people are kind to you...If you see it in your mind, you can hold it in your hand."*

— Steve Harvey

W hen an individual makes a definite decision to manifest their dream life and learns of the universal laws governing their success in life, a natural question that emerges is, "How do I communicate with the universe in a manner that guarantees positive mani-festation instead of negative ones?"

Suppose you're beginning to wonder the same. In that case, whether there's a foolproof way of ensuring you attract the presence of what you desire rather than its continued absence, I have good news for you: you can do two simple things to start signaling to the universe you're ready for your good. The first is creating a vacuum in the area you wish to see the manifestation, and the second is performing the powerful practice of gratitude.

## How to Create a Vacuum for Prosperity

Here's something you must always bear in mind: you are a co-creator in the story of your life. The universe works because you work with the universe. As a co-creator, you take certain steps to set things in motion. Creating space for the good you want to manifest is one of those steps, and cannot be ignored or skipped over.

Countless people on our planet claim they feel lone-liness and say they wish they could have their dream relationship. Some pay for classes or coaching on relationships and read books like this one, but nothing happens. They get an intellectual understanding of the immense power of the law of attraction and the other universal laws. Still, they never accept the responsibility of the co-creator. As such, nothing fully manifests. That relationship they desire remains wishful thinking, not because the law of attraction failed but because they communicate the wrong signals to the universe. A lonely woman who hasn't been in a loving relationship for five years cannot and will not meet the love of her life until she creates space for the new man.

Think about it this way: if you're in your living room, looking at your television set and wishing you had a new one, the first thing you'd need to do is get rid of that old one to make space for a new one. You can't mount a new TV on that spot unless the first one is gone. Am I right? When we speak of physical things, it's easy to see the importance of creating space for something new, but do you know that concept applies to every area of life? That woman who has been lonely for five years is holding on to the idea of her last relationship. Until a woman longing for a relationship lets go and forms a prosperity vacuum, there's nothing for the universe to fill. The universe abhors a vacuum and will have no trouble filling up any space you create mentally and physically.

Still, you've got to make the space. This is what the vacuum law of prosperity is about. It signals to the universe you're in a state of expectancy for something to fill that space.

Catherine Ponder describes how this practice worked in her life and the people to whom she taught prosperity secrets. Some used this principle to furnish their home while others used it to heal from illness. She also tells of her personal story where she gave away most of her clothes to her sister. Upon actually letting them go, she received the gift of new clothes far better than what she previously owned.

The key to making this principle work is to practice forgiveness and learn to fully detach from the lesser good so you can have a greater good. In the earlier example of a woman desiring a relationship, she needs to forgive and let go of her last relationship, then take inspired action to prove she is really in the state of receiving a new relationship.

The nuances of that action will vary from person to person. What matters is that it's an act you believe demonstrates that you now possess your new good.

In addition to creating space for the manifestation in your life and using forgiveness to let go (especially where strong negative emotions are concerned), you should also learn to give and receive.

Give and expect to receive to solidify the signal you're transmitting to the universe.

Even if you're a generous person, receiving can be tough. After all, society teaches us to be givers, but hardly anyone encourages receiving. Give what you have freely, and we all have something we can share with others. If you're low on money, start by giving your time, energy, talent, skills, affection, or the things you own that others might find valuable. But as you give, always do so from a place of love and generosity. Don't give to get something back, as that is counterproductive. You need to learn to give because you feel connected to abundance, even if you don't yet see abundance in the particular area you wish to manifest something new. Let me give you an example.

Suppose you're low on money and your desire is to manifest a large sum so you can finally establish your dream business. In the area of money, you may not be abundant, so your "giving" should be in the area of your life where abundance is expressing itself. Maybe you have a beautiful garden people always admire. So, consider sharing that abundance in whatever way you feel inspired (e.g., cut some of your roses and surprise your elderly neighbor with a bouquet or cook a meal with your veggies and feed your community members). Perhaps you're great at leading a healthy lifestyle. Is there anything you can do to help someone who is in need in that area?

Start where you are and find what you've already got. And trust me, we always have something we can give. The idea here is to use the substance at hand to demonstrate to yourself that you are an abundant being. As you give, keep your mind expectant that somehow the universe shall supply you with more substance.

## How Gratitude and Praise Open Up a Direct Line with the Universe

Appreciation is one of the highest emotional states we can experience. It is perhaps one of the best ways to signal you are in the flow of abundance to the universe. The thing with gratitude and appreciation is that people tend to think that they are effects or outcomes to be experienced after a manifestation occurs. "When I get that dream job, then I'll be happy" or "When I meet the love of my life, then I'll feel love and joy." A common statement I used to hear while growing up was, "When I get rich, then I won't be stressed and I'll finally find happiness."

Unfortunately, these statements go against the natural laws of success. Emotional states never come as the by-product of any manifestations; instead, manifestations are the by-product of certain emotional states. Listen, if you hate your current job, boss or spouse, you'll likely hate the next one too.

If you're not happy right now, I guarantee your future is also full of unhappiness. I'm neither a prophet nor a naysayer; I just understand that the law of attraction cannot give you what you're not. And the way to guarantee a happy future is to begin cultivating joy in the present moment. There's no habit more powerful to the human mind than the habit of daily gratitude. It's like a direct line to the universe that signals you're in the flow of positive abundance. When you're out of flow, no amount of affirmation, visualization, or acts of charity will signal to the universe you're ready for more good. You need to feel gratitude in the present moment regardless of what you have (or don't have). That's how you send the most powerful signal to the universe, and it must respond accordingly.

Meister Eckhart said, "If the only prayer you ever say in your entire life is thank you, it would be enough." Enough for what, exactly? Enough for everything! Each time you feel (really feel) and say, "I really appreciate that" or "I'm grateful for that," you're literally moving energy and vibrating in the state of allowing.

## Why Gratitude Is the Most Potent Manifesting Practice You Can Implement

The high frequency of appreciation and gratitude causes you to vibrate in a state of positive expectation and allow it all without effort or strain. You don't even need to think about details of the specific desire at this point; the fact that you're in the state of gratitude means you're not creating any resistance or barriers to your prosperity, and that's all one needs for the universe to work in their favor. That is, when experiencing the state of gratitude, worry, anxiety, fear, or doubt cannot exist in the mind simultaneously, which means the signal transmitted aligns with positive manifestations. Hence, every second spent appreciating and feeling gratitude for anything at all is really an investment in the full manifestation of your desire.

Of course, you could fall back into doubt as soon as the gratitude feeling dissipates or the external thing causing you to feel appreciation is taken away. And that would block the abundance signals again and drop you back into lesser vibrations. No one expects you to get it right all the time; you just need to fall, then quickly get back up. That's why at the end of this chapter, I'm sharing simple ideas that can help you raise your emotional frequency and maintain this state of gratitude longer.

## The Key to Feeling Grateful for Anything and Everything

The easiest way to have access to gratitude throughout the day is to activate an abundance mindset. If you learn to see the world through the lens of abundance, you'll find abundance already exists all around you. Think about the air you breathe. Where does it come from? How come it never runs out even if you walk into a room full of people? If you're walking past a tree, pause for a moment and observe it. How many leaves can you see? Can you count them all? Are you shopping for groceries right now? Slow down and take notice of the aisles and the abundance of products in that store. So many choices and plenty of evidence of abundance. You don't need to "have" all that stuff to feel abundant; you just need to recognize that it is already here, and you are connected to that same current. There's no trick or gimmick here—this is about increasing your awareness and learning to perceive abundance right where you stand. If you're worried you're not doing it right, trust me, that's just your ego resisting change. There is no right or wrong way of "feeling grateful" in life.

# How to Cultivate Gratitude in Your Life

## The 5-Minute Gratitude Journaling Technique

Take 5 minutes every morning to write down what you appreciate in life. Even if you're currently unemployed or surviving on government handouts, there's something you can feel grateful for, like the fact that you still have a roof over your head and can even afford to read this book. Big or small, writing down anything and everything you know is a blessing will connect you to that state of gratitude.

## Find 3 People Today and Give Them a Compliment

Not only does praising another out loud make that person feel good, but it also amplifies your positive mood and puts you in a state of gratitude and appreciation.

## Look for the Good in All Situations

I know this is hard, especially when it seems nothing good is happening. And that's where you'll need to take a playful, childlike approach to life. As you go about in the world, appreciate the people, nature, buildings, and things you interact with. If a barista gives you extra cream on the house, acknowledge the good in that gesture. If the traffic lights open up just in time for you to avoid traffic and make your meeting, recognize that moment as well. These seemingly random "lucky" occurrences are tiny sparks placed on our journey to enable us to tap back into the current of good, so don't overlook them.

# Learn to Make a Big Deal of the Small Blessings and Successes in Your Life

Often, we downplay small blessings and exaggerate minor mishaps, which only pushes us further away from our dream life. Perhaps a waiter got your order wrong this morning, which put you in a foul mood, leading to an argument that messed up the rest of your day. By the time you got home, you'd told everyone about that horrible waiter. That's an entire day of negative signals sent out to the universe. But just maybe, you could have made a different choice. You could have focused on the lady who held the door open for you or the new colleague who covered for you when they realized you were late handing in your project.

Our brains can jeopardize our desires simply because the ego gets inflated and dwells too much on the wrongs instead of celebrating what's working. So, do a self-analysis and take note of how quickly you get over something good in your life and how long you dwell on failure or negative experiences. Sometimes, this one shift unlocks all the good that's been blocked over the years.

Remember, you can't be worried or pessimistic and grateful at the same time. When sending out the right signals, if the only job you give yourself is maintaining an attitude of gratitude, you will see improvement in all areas of your life. And yes, that will enable the law of attraction to match you with the desire you already ordered.

# Chapter 14

## The Missing Ingredient for Manifestation That No One Talks About

*"What you radiate outward in your thoughts, feelings, mental pictures, and words, you attract into your life."*

— Catherine Ponder

An often-overlooked aspect of manifesting is alignment. Many of us fail to realize that at any given moment, we are going through life in harmony or out of harmony with the laws of success. When we disobey the universal laws, no amount of action or prayer can bring about the manifestation we desire because an out-of-alignment being tends to operate in counter-opposition to their good.

Think about the difference demonstrated in the following scenario. Two employees are working in the sales department for the same organization. Both desire to hit the same financial goal at the end of the first quarter. They have similar training, strong work ethics, and are equally willing to do everything possible to close five new accounts that would bring in a significant revenue stream to their organization and seal their bonus for the year. There are also rumors of a promotion opening up at the end of the year. Both individuals feel they'd be perfect for the leadership role. So, it's game on for these men, and over the weeks leading up to the end of the quarter, one can hardly see a significant difference in their output. However, at the end of the quarter, results proved that one of the guys hit his bull's eye while the other barely made it past the halfway point. How could this be when both men put in so much effort?

Throughout this book, we've mentioned the importance of alignment in the process of manifesting desire. Action is essential in manifesting, but no amount of activity can substitute alignment. This topic is so vital to your success, it warrants dedicating a short chapter to clarify what alignment means and how to align yourself with your desire.

# What Do We Mean When We Speak of Alignment?

Alignment means having your thoughts, emotions, imagination, and therefore your vibrational offering "in flow" and operating in a manner that harmonizes with the laws of success.

Alignment isn't something you can fake or force. It's also not something you do once and forget about. Flow is an ongoing moment-by-moment process. At any given point during your day, you can get into alignment as your energy rises, or fall out of alignment as your energy dips.

Most of us live from the outside-in, so our day is a constant fluctuation. We see someone we love, a funny cat video, or an inspiring talk from a guru, and alignment occurs for those few moments. Half an hour later, while driving home, a driver cuts us off and our anger brews. We then see something in the news and despair kicks in, taking us out of alignment.

Have you ever had the following experience? You wake up in the morning, go through your morning routine feeling good, and by the time you sit down for breakfast, someone texts you bad news...and all that good feeling suddenly goes out the window? That's an experience of being in alignment and being out of alignment. Unfortunately, every time you're out of alignment, you're moving further away from the good you desire. The gap in frequency between where you are and where you dream of being continues to grow. On the flip side, every time you're in alignment, the gap shrinks, and as you move toward your desire, it moves towards you. Any action you take from that place of alignment will prove extremely valuable.

Abraham Hicks once got a question from an audience member who asked how she could win the winning lottery ticket. Her desire was to manifest a lot of money (she didn't specify how much) and proclaimed she didn't want to work hard to manifest this cash; instead, she preferred to win the lottery. The audience cheered upon hearing this question, and I must admit, even I got curious to hear how Abraham would respond.

After a momentary silence, his response came: "You can't win the lottery!" The room went dead silent. You could see the woman's face turning pale as despair kicked in.

"But you said the law of attraction works on anything, Abraham. Why can't it work on my desire?" retorted the woman. And that's when Abraham went into a lengthy rant about energetic alignment.

The short summary of Abraham's teaching was this: if you have a desire to manifest money and go out into the world totally out of alignment, any action you take will only cause you grief. It won't bring you any closer to your money. Your boss won't pay you enough, the lottery cards you buy won't be the winning tickets, and so on. And by the way, buying a ticket because you're desperate to find the winning number works against the laws of success. When disobeying universal laws, all you get is heartache and greater suffering. Conversely, when you've done the work and you're energetically aligned (in your flow), anything and everything becomes an active channel to your good.

## Closing the Vibrational Gap

By now, you should be operating from the understanding that you are first and foremost a vibrational being in constant communication with the universe.

If you're still in doubt, that's what you need to work on before moving forward. As a vibrational being, you're either moving toward your desire or away from it (depending on how aligned you are). This gap is something our conscious mind can sense; that's why we often say things like "How do I get from here to there?" or "I know what to do, and I understand the law of attraction, but it's not working for me." These are all statements that reveal a huge vibrational gap between you and the desire currently existing as a spiritual prototype on a specific vibrational frequency to which you lack access.

An old analogy that might make sense to those who grew up pre-internet and Apple Music is that of radio stations. Back in the day, if I wanted to listen to a particular radio station, e.g., WBLS 107.5, I literally had to turn a knob or press a little button until I landed on that specific frequency. The further away I was (if it was previously at 87.9), the longer it would take to reach my desired frequency. But regardless of how far or close my tuner was, I could go all the way up and access my favorite station with a little deliberate intention. And even if I was listening to KBHN-Power 87.9 and hating it, WBLS 107.5 still existed, and they were playing all my favorite jams. I just didn't have access yet. Does this make sense?

# How Do I Spend More Time in Alignment?

This is the golden question, and perhaps the only discussion that matters once you get alignment. And the answer is simple: notice when you feel in alignment, then acknowledge and feel deep gratitude for being in alignment. In other words, make a big deal out of those moments when you find yourself in alignment and try to extend that time as far as you can. Then when you realize you're out of alignment, don't beat yourself up about it. Too many good LOA students punish themselves when they wake up in alignment and fall off by the time they get to work. They then spend the rest of the morning and afternoon pissed off at everything and everyone (including themselves) for falling off their alignment. That negative thought or anger that rushed in and spoiled your perfect Zen morning is not the reason you're out of alignment six hours later. The reason you're out of alignment is that you're still fixating on what happened earlier in the day or earlier in the week (or ten years ago).

Here's a golden take-home point you might want to highlight in your private journal: alignment is an ongoing process. Your present alignment is the only thing that matters relative to your manifestation. It doesn't really matter how often you fall out of alignment, especially when working on your energy levels. What matters is that you quickly pick yourself up again, make peace with the negative emotions or painful experiences, and quickly shift your attention back to what you desire.

## Make Peace with Negative Emotion

Our physical human existence requires us to accept that duality is part of the game. The law of polarity is ever in operation. The only reason we can detect something hot is that cold exists. If sadness wasn't part of the emotional scale, we would never truly know what happiness feels like. Humans fail to understand that negative emotions are not the cause of suffering. Rather, our ignorance of the purpose they serve is the real culprit.

Think of having a car that didn't have a fuel gauge or a computer that didn't have a battery icon. As I write this, my laptop battery gives me indications of how much energy it has before I must plug it in for refueling. If I ignore it or get angry about the warning signal to plug it in for recharging, I won't write anymore. Worse still, I could lose all my unsaved work. That's why we all love the indicators on our gadgets and cars that let us know when we need to pay attention. How is it that we appreciate the value of having those beeping indicators yet struggle to see the value of negative emotion? Is it because we don't fully understand that we're vibrational beings first and foremost, and that our true nature is joy?

Make peace with all the areas of your life that don't seem to be "just right" and learn to appreciate that even those lower frequencies serve a purpose. It is your job and duty to become more deliberate about where you place your attention and how you feel. Once you've set your eyes on something good that makes you come alive, invest as much energy as you can, raising your energy and vibrational frequency. Use tools, practices, affirmations, and anything else that influences your energy. And when you fall to a lower frequency and land on despair, anger, powerlessness, or frustration, don't beat yourself up or dwell on it. Do what you'd do if your car's fuel alarm went off: shift your focus into fixing it. For the vehicle, the simple solution is to stop at the nearest gas station and add more fuel. With your mind-body-spirit connection, the simple solution is to build bridge thoughts that enable you to rise in frequency.

We'll be talking about other techniques you can use to raise your vibration in the second to last chapter, and we have a whole section on meditations that can also boost your frequency. As you can see, alignment isn't complicated or elusive. It just requires discipline and the proper perspective.

## Chapter 15

---

# Two Phases of Manifesting and Attraction

*"To desire is to expect, to expect is to achieve."*

— Raymond Holliwell

I n his book, author and metaphysical teacher Raymond Holliwell said that to align best with the law of attraction, we must under-stand both desire and expectation.

Holliwell teaches that:

These mental attitudes represent lines of attractive force, the former being the positive phase of the law and the latter the negative phase... The first phase of "desire" embraces a positive process of attraction; that is, when an individual earnestly desires a thing, he sets up a line of force that connects him with the invisible side of the good desired. Should he weaken or change in his desire, that particular line of force is disconnected or misses its goal; but if he remains constant in his desire or ambition, the good demanded is sooner or later realized in part or in entirety. The principle involved is that you cannot long or year for anything unless it already exists, if not in form, then in substance, and "desire" is the motive power for calling it forth into visible appearance or physical effect. (*Working With The Law*, Hollowell, 1964, p.43)

It's worth reading this passage several times until it becomes clear in your mind that your work isn't just to desire something, as that's only half the equation. The other half is that you must expect it. Expectations are usually our stumbling blocks (yet we tend to blame lack of materialization on the law of attraction). So let's devote a little time to working out how to start expecting the right way.

Imagine you woke up early one morning, thrilled to go fishing in the sea. You packed up, drove all the way, set yourself up right, adhered to all the proper protocols, even paddled to just the right spot. You excitedly threw your fishing rod with the bait in the water and just sat there waiting...an hour went by, then another and another. All the while, a big-sized fish with your hook trapped in its mouth suffered in anguish as it waited for you to reel it in! After six hours of waiting, you grew tired, weary, and eventually passed out from exhaustion.

All this time, both you and the trapped fish stood at an impasse because you weren't willing to do your half of the job and reel in the catch. Left to your own devices, you'd sit there and die—thirsty, hungry, and without fish. The poor fish would also lose because it's not strong enough to unhook itself. In the end, it would be a loss on both ends, all because you didn't finish the job. You might laugh at the silliness of this story, but many personal development students are doing this with their desires. They do everything right, but they never reel in their catch. And how does one "reel in the fish"? Through expectation.

When you desire an income of 10,000 or 20,000 dollars a month, but you don't expect it, you're simply wasting valuable mental energy. I know so many people who desire to be healed from disease, promoted at work, or get pregnant after trials and trials of failure. When I dig deeper, I usually find that although these individuals desire good things to happen, they often make little to no effort to positively expect the materialization of their good. Some might even say, I've been unemployed for too many years and I've applied to so many job openings, but no one is hiring. That, right there, is the poison leaking out. That individual desires to be employed, but they expect not to get a job they'd want. At best, they'd get a job that frustrates them.

Expectation is powerful. It's the thing that seals your deals. And I can bet anything that if you've struggled to manifest anything in recent years, it's mainly because you didn't check in with yourself to understand where your expectations were rooted. You might be talking "riches" but expecting "poverty." You may desire a new business, but you might be expecting no sales or "hardships." The law never fails your expectations.

How to get on the right side of the law of attraction through positive expectations:

Have you ever seen a cat waiting patiently and intently for a mouse to come out of its hole? If so, then you've witnessed positive expectations first-hand. That cat expects to catch its prize at any moment. It remains calm and alert, patient yet persistent, believing that the mouse will eventually come out of its hole.

But here's the thing: if that cat started doubting or lost interest in her prize, her energy would show, and sooner rather than later, she would be distracted by something else. The same can be said regarding your "prize." Whatever you desire to manifest should build up your keen interest and attention just as you witness with the cat waiting to catch the mouse. That interest is intensified with anticipation of the full materialization of your price. As you sit in that "knowing" that it is yours and coming about at any moment, you draw to you the success and steps necessary to meet it halfway.

So what am I saying here? To reel in your manifestation, you need to turn up the volume of your attention and interest to build positive expectations. Here's an example of what that might look like in real life.

My younger sister came to me a few months ago anxious about the layoffs in her organization. She feared her entire department would be downsized significantly. All her colleagues already had one foot out the door as they anticipated the fateful news. She asked me, "What should I do?" I suggested that if she loves working at the organization, she should hold her attention and interest there. The daily work she does should be exceptional. Her attitude should become optimistic, and she should see herself growing within the organization not getting fired. I then proceeded to teach her the basics you've learned throughout this book. After we identified her burning desire, the task was to maintain a state of positive expectation.

My sister went off immediately to implement all the instructions I gave her with great care and commitment. She exceeded what we'd talked about. Three months later, she phoned me shrieking with excitement because senior leadership had called her in for a meeting in which they described the changes they wished to make within the organization. A new leadership position was opening, and they wanted her to take on that challenge. Not only did my sister not get laid off, but she also got a raise and a new position at a time when everyone else was expecting the worst.

If you don't understand how the game of life works and how to align with your desires, it will appear as though bad things happen to good people. But in the case of my sister's story, her colleagues were already expecting to receive that termination letter. They were already job-hunting and taking interviews else-where. All the while, my sister was sinking her roots deeper into the organization, using her skills and talents to show how valuable she was to such a company. It was only a matter of time before the law of attraction matched everyone with the conditions that fit their expectations.

If you desire better health, a romantic partner, more money, or happiness, you can wish and desire all you want, but the fact is, you'll only manifest and enjoy as much or as little as you genuinely expect. When you set a goal for more money and fear, and doubt your ability to earn that amount, you vibrate out of alignment with the very thing you want. Your mental forces are weakened, and you can only attract the conditions that match up with your lesser beliefs and negative expectations. See how this works?

# Vibrating in Your Knowing

Abraham Hicks says, "You can't cease to vibrate, and the law of attraction will not stop responding to the vibration that you're offering. So, expansion is inevitable. You provide it, whether you know you do or not."

But how can you vibrate in the knowing that "reels in" your desire? How do you stabilize that positive expectation?

By creating leverage for yourself.

In the business world, leverage is the best-kept secret for business success. Smart business owners are constantly looking for ways to create leverage because they know it directly impacts their revenue and business longevity. The same is true in your world. By identifying ways to create the kind of leverage that enables you to stabilize positive expectations, you're guaranteed to maintain alignment with the frequency of your desire even if you're not directly focusing on the objective.

The only way to get leverage is by learning how to spend most of your day in vibrational harmony. The more you can focus your attention on things, people, experiences, and actions that keenly excite your interests, the easier it becomes to sustain a frequency that works in your favor. You can retrain your thought patterns and emotions into vibrational harmony by consciously choosing actions and behaviors that enable you to vibrate in your knowing.

A young man I know very well and shall always prize as a friend has demonstrated the power of vibrating in one's knowing superbly. By the time he hit his early twenties, he had already been promoted to the C-suite at the company he worked for. Today, at age 29, he is the Regional Vice President and the youngest at the organization to have reached such high rankings in the firm's history. When I asked him how he's manifested this dream career that seems almost magical, he said, "I enjoy my work, and I'm very interested in learning and growing, so I push myself to ever greater heights at each opportunity. The advancements just come without me having to worry or fret about it." When I dug deeper into his childhood and upbringing, it became clear that he was imbued with the paradigm that naturally enabled him to align with the law of attraction since early childhood. He's not lucky; instead, he vibrates in his knowing, and that allows him to manifest better and better in every domain of his life with seeming effortlessness.

That's what you must learn to do in your life. The more you can focus your attention on actions that enable you to amplify your interests and direct your thinking into constructive, positive ideas, the more good you will attract into your life.

Emerson once said, "See how the mass of men worry themselves into nameless graves, while here and there a great unselfish soul forgets himself into immortality." That is the great unlock for anyone who wants to manifest their dream lifestyle. Give your attention wholeheartedly to the thing at hand that raises your highest interests and focus on your values first. What do I mean here? Suppose your highest value is honesty. Your main job is to vibrate in that knowing because that's the principle you guide yourself by. Tame your mind to support this value in all you do, think, and feel. At work, you need to do your best honest work. Should you get an opportunity to deceive or steal in any way, shape, or form, stick to your values and refuse to take advantage of anything (no matter how trivial) that contradicts your principles. Watch yourself closely, and you'll come to see how often you betray your own truth each day. And suppose you discover that you're constantly falling off your values. In that case, you cannot maintain vibrational harmony, let alone rise in frequency to a new and higher state.

# What If I Don't Know My Values and Guiding Principles?

That becomes the main immediate work. If you don't know your values, you have no way of shaping and directing your mind. Without a tamed mind, the law of attraction will always seem to be unreliable and capricious. There will be no consistency because you don't consistently vibrate in harmony with the good you desire. So, start by identifying the core values that must guide your life. Commit to living from that knowing and focus on ensuring this is demonstrated in your current lifestyle. As you do, things will start expanding. Your interest will continue to grow, and your frequency will rise steadily until you match up with everything you set as the next level of manifestation in your dream life.

From this point on, we'll focus more on taking the initiative than dwelling on the theory of the law of attraction because in the end, what matters is your ability to apply knowledge gained.

## Managing Your Vibrational Alignment

If there's one takeaway I really want you to grasp from this chapter, it's that you don't have to waste mental energy forcing yourself to think about money, being rich, or meeting that special someone—especially if thinking about the specificity of the desire only throws you off alignment. For someone who grew up in abject poverty, thinking about earning $20,000 each month is actually harder to both visualize and maintain positive expectations. They would think of money and feel its absence. The better solution is to focus on an interest that raises their vibration, identify a value or principle they want to live by, and start where they are to do everything possible to live from that heightened state of interest and living in alignment with their knowing. As they do, the money and any other desired thing will come.

So if you've struggled to manifest something you've never had in your life, this is good news for you—you don't need to focus on that specific desire. Once you've set it as your goal and followed the steps outlined in chapter 6, detach from the particular desire and do this instead:

## Focus on the present moment.

Your power lies in this present moment. The future experience you'll encounter is created at this moment based on how you feel and what you're thinking. So, it's time to become more present. You'll find your thoughts wandering to events that happened in the past or worrying about what will happen in the future. As you catch yourself, gently guide your mind as you would a little child and bring it back to this moment by giving it something highly engaging to focus on. The more you learn to lovingly get your thoughts back to the present moment, the easier it will be to control your emotions, and that's what we want more of.

## Increase your self-control so you can limit talking about what you don't want with others.

We are all so guilty of this habit, yet all it does is poison our dreams. Think about how often you've felt wronged or hurt by someone and wasted hours, if not days, dwelling on that moment. You called a friend and discussed it some more, replayed the scenario over and over in your mind, went to bed thinking about it, and awoke the next only to pick up that mental argument with the person yet again. All this does is add fuel to negative emotions and throw you out of whack. The antidote is simple: learn to drop unwanted emotions like hot potatoes. These unwanted vibrations are the signals you send to the universe, and they are what the law of attraction responds to. So, don't indulge in negative conversations in your thinking or with friends any longer. Your dreams suffer when you do.

**Start feeling and thinking like the person (the version of you) who is already living in the reality of your manifestation.**

Imagine how you will feel and how the world looks from this new vantage point.

Here are some powerful questions to ask yourself each morning:

- *What is that version of me thinking and feeling today?*

- *How would he/she prioritize this day?*
- *What kind of problems is he/she solving?*
- *What kind of actions is he/she taking?*
- *Who do I need to become today to match that me?*

# Chapter 16

## Tools and Techniques for Manifesting Your Dream Life

*"You create your own universe as you go along."*

— Winston Churchill

Here is a list of manifesting techniques to add to your toolbox of life. Some might work better than others. I recommend testing one technique at a time for at least three times before determining whether it works for you or not. Remember, faith has a lot to do with the effectiveness of these tools, so keep cultivating that faith.

# The Generalizing Technique

This Abraham Hicks-inspired technique is excellent for manifesting anything, especially financial abundance. Why? Because finances tend to have a huge emotional sting (primarily negative), which typically makes it hard to shift to a higher frequency. Most people actually repel money when they focus on manifesting money. So if you're having a hard time manifesting, and you can feel there's plenty of resistance around that subject, consider using this technique to bring you back into alignment.

First, accept the current circumstances that have caused you to experience the negative emotion and experience. Acknowledge them and how they make you feel, but don't give them your power.

The second thing to do is to take the negative emotion or experience as evidence that your beliefs are out of alignment with your desire. You want to attract something good, but you're experiencing the opposite. It's not because the law of attraction has failed you, but because you're operating at a frequency that's in direct opposition with the good you want. See how important this step is? You're getting signals from the universe through your emotions so you can "wake up" and take actions that will shift your current vibrational state. Once you truly realize this fact, it's time to move on.

The third thing to do is generalize the negative emotions to take the sting out of them. Take the next small step upward in your emotional scale. For example, if you're worried about money, your goal shouldn't be to feel rich and joyful; that wouldn't last very long. Instead, the goal is to go general to the point you feel a little overwhelmed and possibly start to feel bored. Once you're bored, it's easy to bump yourself up to contentment, and then you can quickly begin to rise to higher frequencies.

Suppose you're stuck in worry about paying bills. At this level, the law of attraction is far from serving you the riches you want. Instead of thinking about becoming a millionaire and obsessing about affirmations, work on tuning into a slightly better feeling like overwhelm (believe it or not, this is a better feeling for someone worried). Feeling overwhelmed by the extra work you might have to do to earn more money is a higher vibration than worry. And as you think about the job, don't get into the details of what kind of work; just stay as general as you can: "I need more money, so I need to get more work..." Accept this fact and keep reaching for a higher feeling and more generalized thoughts until you land on the feeling of contentment. This example is a simple illustration of going general around the topic that's creating an emotional sting until that feeling dissipates.

## Mindfulness Appreciation Technique

This technique is a mindfulness practice that can almost be viewed as a form of meditation in which we'll fuse the act of praise and appreciation with mindfulness. I recommend doing this practice daily, just before bed or immediately upon waking up.

Start with a few deep breaths. Four counts inhale, and four counts exhale. Relax your body and bring your awareness to this moment. Think of a person, pet, or anything else that has recently supported your journey toward abundance or success in any area of life that matters to you. Suppose one of your goals was healing from a particular disease. In that case, the doctor you worked with, the nurse, a friend who drove you to the hospital, or even your pet can all be considered relevant. The subject matter isn't important; what matters is that you express appreciation to them both logically and emotionally.

This practice is an extremely powerful technique when done with heartfelt intention because you can carry over the vibration it builds to other areas of your life. If you practice this technique daily, you'll create a momentum that the law of attraction will respond to with adequate evidence.

# The Manifestation Box Technique

This technique allows you to manifest whatever your heart desires through written messages, pictures, and other ideas that represent your desires. I like to think of it as direct mailing to the universe. Here's how to do it.

First, you want to make a magical box. Consider turning a shoebox, jewelry box, or a regular container into a magic box. Color it up and add some sparkles or whatever else causes you to look at it in a special way. Place this magical box somewhere specific in the house, and then place whatever you want inside it. As you place something inside it, the universe receives the signal and responds with a physical representation of your desire. Consider using magazine cutouts that resemble your desires, quotes you make from scratch, written affirmations, scripts, heirlooms, gifts, or crystals to communicate your desire. Anything that represents the energy you wish to receive will always be a suitable representation to add to the box.

## The Clarity through Contrast Technique

This is another Abraham Hicks original and I often use it because of how simple yet powerful it is. If you're setting new goals or have trouble identifying what you want to manifest next, this exercise will save you time and set you on the right frequency fast.

Begin by folding an A4 paper in half. On the left side, write "Contrast." On the right side, write "Clarity."

Under the "Contrast" headline, write all the things you don't want, such as "I don't want to struggle to pay my bills." Under "Clarity," you write what the opposite of that would be. In this case, it is: "I want to have an abundance of financial supply so I can always pay my bills on time."

Continue writing everything you don't want and follow it up with the extreme opposite as best as you can. For many people, the best approach to identifying desires and goals is, to begin with, what they are currently aware they don't want. That's why this technique is so effective. But once you've clearly written down with clarity what you want, tear the left half of the paper and shred it, symbolizing that you've let go of that old state. Refocus on your energy on the right half of your paper and start "feeling" what it would be like to be and have what you clearly wrote down.

## The 55x5 Technique

This technique is simple yet extremely powerful when it comes to reconstructing your subconscious mind. Through the 55x5 technique, you'll work on changing your subconscious patterns of belief over five days.

Begin by choosing an affirmation that profoundly resonates with you, something you feel certain speaks to the abundant lifestyle you want to manifest. Make sure the affirmation is something you can easily memorize and tis detailed enough without stirring up your inner resistance. I also want you to ensure the affirmation is in the present-tense first-person. For example, "I am a successful business owner."

Do you have your affirmation now? Good. The next thing to do is write this affirmation (by hand) 55 times in a row for five consecutive days. Grab your pen and paper or journal and begin now. Practice present-moment awareness as you do this and make sure you've engaged your emotions. As you write each word, you should be feeling something—it's that simple. For example, suppose your affirmation is, "I am in a loving, passionate, committed, and healthy relationship with my soulmate." In that case, the emotions you want to feel as you write out the statement 55 times might include warmth, tenderness, love, joy, etc. The more feelings you bring to this exercise, the more powerful it will be.

Once you have successfully completed five days in a row, it's time to practice the law of detachment we discussed earlier in the book. Let go and trust that the universe knows exactly how to match you up and deliver your manifestation. As a gesture of your detachment and letting go, consider taking all the pieces of paper with the written affirmations and placing them in an envelope, then put them some-where safe. Tell yourself you've left them there for the universe to take care of. Come back to them once you've manifested the desire.

## The Focus Wheel Technique

I first learned this technique from Catherine Ponder, who taught the incredible effects this simple exercise had brought her students. The exercise is quite simple, but extremely effective when shifting vibrational states. It enables you to focus more on positive thoughts and attitudes in relation to your desires.

To practice this technique, begin by grabbing a plain A4 paper and drawing a small circle in the center. In that center, write what you want, e.g., "good health." Next, write down an optimistic belief you have about that subject matter. Place the words around the edge of the central circle. In the case of good health, a thought that might be true even for you could be "Being healthy is something everyone deserves, including me." Keep going and write as many positive beliefs you have around this topic. Go around that circle, and if you keep writing, your page will be full of statements supporting the reality and naturalness of what you wish to manifest. By the time you've filled that page, your vibrational knowing will be completely different, and the law of attraction will start responding to that. It's that simple.

## The Placemat Technique

The placemat technique is another Abraham Hicks favorite that works exceptionally well if you're stuck at feeling overwhelm and can't seem to move your way up the emotional scale. Here's how to do it.

Grab a piece of paper the size of a placemat. Draw a line down the middle of the paper. On one side, label it *"Things for me to do,"* and on the other, label it *"Things for the universe to do for me."*

Now, dump everything onto that paper that's been stressing you. Give the universe most of the heavy-lifting work you feel incapable of doing on your own. Allow yourself to turn these big tasks over to the universe. Once you feel completely emptied out and relieved that the universe is clear on what you need help with, trust in the process. Know that the universe has your back and carry that paper with you over the following days, weeks, and months until each action is taken care of. Repeat this exercise as often as needed.

# The Dimension-Jumping Technique

This particular technique is especially cool for those who love science or sci-fi shows. It is, however, a highly advanced technique, so I encourage you to do it only after you feel confident in your knowledge of the law of attraction. The exercise is based on quantum physics, more precisely, the theory known as the many-worlds theory. In quantum mechanics, the many-worlds interpretation asserts that the universal wavefunction is objectively real and there is no wavefunction collapse. That implies that all possible outcomes of quantum measurements are physically realized in some "world" or universe (source: Wikipedia). Perhaps an easier way for sci-fi lovers to get this is to think of the multiverse.

In simple layman's terms, what I understand is that we live in an infinite universe, and each action has an endless number of possibilities and realities. Everything that can happen does happen in different realities. And so, a manifestation technique that can enable you to jump from one reality to another should be pretty cool, right? Of course, there's no concrete evidence of this in physical science, but we have all the know-how we need to test out the validity of this concept as spiritually awakened beings.

Suppose your desire is money and you'd like to double your income in the next 30 days. Currently, you're sitting in a reality that has the absence of money. So if you'd like to use this technique to manifest the presence of money, you'll need two cups, a few Post-It notes, a pen, and water.

Start by placing two Post-It notes in front of you. On one, write "current situation," and on the other, write "desired situation." Describe each situation in as much detail and length as you wish. Once you feel satisfied with your description, stick each Post-It note on an empty glass. You now have one glass representing the current absence and one representing the presence of your desire.

The next thing to do is pour water into the "current situation" glass and see the words you wrote in your mind's eye. Place your hands around the glass as though you were pouring your energy and vision into it. Summon your creative abilities and use imagination and visualization in this exercise if you desire the best results. Feel yourself poured into the glass and becoming one with the water.

Once you feel you've complete this action, take that glass of water and pour it into the "desired situation" glass. Once again, place your hands around the glass and feel yourself one with the water in this new desired state. In your mind's eye, see the words you wrote and enter the vivid reality of that outcome. Notice how your energy and the water have now shifted as you immerse yourself in this new reality. Soak in these new feelings for as long as possible. When you feel complete and anchored in that new state, drink the water to the very last drop. Allow yourself to continue feeling these good feelings and trust that you have shifted dimensions.

Before you go about seeing the world through a new lens, discard the "current situation" Post-It note. Hold on to the "desired situation" Post-It note, but I recommend crossing out the word "desired" and replacing it with "current" to prove to your mind that your new dimension is actual. And that's it! You just jumped dimensions.

# The "Act as If" Technique

This visualization technique is a game-changer when you learn to do it right. Here's how:

Picture the version of yourself that you will be once you've manifested your desire. Now, go about your day acting as if you are already that person living your dream life. In other words, make-believe that your future is now present-tense. While it may seem hard and "fake" to your adult mind, your inner child will enjoy doing this technique very much. After all, when you were younger, you probably spent most of your time acting as if you were someone or something. Perhaps you acted as though you were your favorite superhero or an astronaut vising space...remember those days? Well, you could be driving an old, beat-up, second-hand Prius and act as if you were driving a MBW 6X latest model. And if your energy is right, your mind wouldn't be able to tell the difference. When you raise your frequency and align with the energy of the person you would love to become, you naturally become that person. The universe also starts responding to you as though you are, in fact, that person. It's as simple as that.

# The Gratitude-Stacking Technique

Gratitude is by far one of the most potent and most effective tools at your disposal if you really want to become a masterful manifester—and I think that's still an understatement. You need to prioritize the practice of gratitude in your daily life. This technique can help you accomplish just that. Here's how to do it.

Begin by listing out on a private journal or paper all the things you're grateful for. Once you've exhausted your current thinking, go back and read everything you put on the paper. As you're reading your list (do this slowly), imbue each word with as much feeling as possible. Allow yourself to reconnect with the "good vibes" that thing you listed gives you. If you're doing this in a safe space, consider reading it aloud and letting your voice amplify the good feelings as you speak with appreciation and heartfelt excitement. If you're in public, that's okay—exaggerate the words in your mind as you mentally shout them aloud with joy. One thing to note is that you should do all your gratitude in the present tense. For example, "Thank you for the air I breathe" or "I am so happy and grateful now that my colleague Bobby and I are finally getting along."

The more things you can stack up to create a mega-gratitude list, the better. You'll vibrate at that frequency of joy quickly when you come up with a list that keeps you going for a while. At the start of this practice, you might only have written down three things, and nothing more. It might take you under a minute to complete. That's okay as long as you soak in that feeling a little while. As you continue to stack up and re-read your list daily, after a little while, you'll find you can take an entire ten minutes just counting all your blessings and deeply feeling that warm, buzzy sensation in the solar plexus. That's when you know you've struck your gold mine.

## The Rampage of Appreciation

This is a powerful technique you can apply in as little as 20 seconds, and you'll already feel the shift in frequency.

Begin by looking at your current environment and identify a person, animal, or object that pleases you. Hold your focus on that person, pet, or thing and notice how good it feels to admire and think about them. Tune into the beauty, usefulness, and goodness you're connected to in this moment as you focus on them. Mentally or even out loud, offer them a compliment, and notice again how good it feels in your body. Once you notice your good feeling is more substantial than when you first began the exercise, move onto another pleasing object and continue this rampage of appreciation.

A simple example of this would be the following:

1. If you own a pet cat, sit with her for a few minutes in the morning before you head to work and use that good feeling to kickstart that momentum.

2. Tell her how much you love her and really connect with that feeling.

3. Get into your car and find another object that makes you feel good. Perhaps this time, find a song that uplifts you. Play the song on repeat the whole way to work, all the while appreciating how good it makes you feel.

4. Once at work, find another object or person, and do your best to string these

moments of appreciation as far into the day as you can.

If, however, you're having a terrible day and feeling down with anxiety or overwhelm, you're better off using other techniques to rise a little higher before this rampage can be effective enough. For example, you could use the "Which Thought Feels Better?" technique below.

## Which Thought Feels Better?

This is a powerful technique when you want to raise your frequency, but are currently stuck in low vibrations.

Start by taking a piece of paper (do this exercise by hand instead of typing) and write down your thoughts. Be honest and suspend self-judgment or guilt. Name the emotion as best as you can. For example, "It seems I feel anxious."

Next, I want you to write a second emotion that might be related to it and evaluate which feels better. If the second word feels better than the first, continue writing down another thought or feeling related to that word that might feel better. Think of this exercise as laying one brick at a time as you build your emotional home. If you realize the word or emotion you picked doesn't make you feel better or perhaps is even worse than the last, reframe it and try again. The intention here isn't to get to joy and freedom; instead, it's about feeling better now than you did an hour ago.

# The Scripting Technique

Can you manifest your dream life just by writing it down? Yes, you can—when done in a specific way. Scripting is the perfect way to express feeling, identify your core desire, and leverage gratitude. By choosing to script your desires, you're engaging in a visualization exercise commonly referred to as future pacing. It's about having what you want in the future, and then reinforcing that new vibrational setpoint by describing the situation in clear and vivid detail. Simply said, it's about writing your future in as much detail as possible as though it's already here and now.

A case study will demonstrate how to do this technique far better than a technical description. So, let me share the story of a life coach named Pascal, who often talks about how he used scripting to manifest his dream house.

When Coach Pascal started scripting, he was bankrupt and on the verge of getting a divorce. Everything seemed to be falling apart, and with nothing left to lose, he surrendered to the universe (typically the best moments for natural laws to really start working). Pascal bought a special book to practice a technique he'd learned from a law of attraction coach. Every morning, he woke up and spent over half an hour scripting his dream life in specific details. Pascal wrote in the present tense the new home he was living in and described it with astonishing detail right down to the color of the tiles in his master bedroom. It was a big two-story home with a beautiful garden and large enough rooms for him to set up a home office and private gym. He described the wonderful morning rituals he and his soulmate would enjoy together and how loving she would be. All this, Pascal scripted out in a book to his heart's content. Once he felt utterly immersed in that world and thrilled to be alive, he would then come back into the current (nightmarish) reality and work hard to sustain those emotions throughout the day. Some days were easier than others, but in every case, he knew that dream life was his destiny.

It took him six years, nine months, and thirteen days to get to that day when he moved into a new home with his new bride. And that home was an identical match to the words scripted in his journal. When he showed the book to his new wife, they both broke down in tears as the divinity of their life and relationship truly dawned on them. That is the power of scripting.

Use scripting to activate your divinity and let your imagination create a life that thrills you. Then, work extra hard to stay true to that script. Your brain will unconsciously start sending vibrational signals to coordinate and align the people, things, opportunities, and resources you need to walk right into that desired future. This is the work I invite you to commit to. Ask yourself, "What would I love to be, have, do, and give? Who must I become to align with that version of myself?" Script it all out until it feels good and natural to you.

The truth is, your life is the way it is now because of the story you're telling yourself every single day. You may not realize this, but you're scripting your reality unconsciously. I'm asking you to become intentional and deliberate that narrative. Take charge. Stop telling it like it is, and start telling it as you would love it to be. Script it, surrender to the universe, and trust the universe has your back. The universe never fails those who believe without a doubt.

# Chapter 17

## Meditations to Boost Your Manifesting Power

*"The universe never asked you to struggle. It is simply answering your mood."*

— Unknown

In this section of the book, you'll receive meditation scripts focused on manifesting more love, happiness, healing, and success so you can create your dream life through the law of attraction. These meditations are aimed at assisting you with transforming all areas of your life, including love and relationships, health and healing, finance, career success, and overall happiness. These meditations range in length between ten and twenty minutes. They will guide you through a process of internal transformation and inspiration. Feel free to focus on the specific mediations that resonate with you most. Remember to enjoy yourself during this process.

## Manifesting Health

For this meditation, get yourself into a relaxed and comfortable position. You may choose to sit comfortably or lie down. Begin by focusing on your breath...inhaling slowly and exhaling slowly. Mentally say to yourself, "Inhaling now," and then as you exhale mentally, say, "Exhaling now." Repeat this several times until you feel keenly focused on your breath, relaxed, and doing deep conscious breathing, repeating the inhaling and exhaling for a few more minutes. As your breathing continues, allow your body to be completely relaxed. Observe the relaxation. Observe the muscles letting go and the tension releasing as you sink into your chair or bed. Relax deeper and deeper with each and every breath. Continue to mentally say, "inhaling now" and "exhaling now."

Feel the body getting heavier and heavier, more and more relaxed. From your head down through your neck, shoulders, arms, hands, then all through the torso down to the hips, legs, feet, and toes—allow every muscle to let go and relax. Feel how good it feels to relax and just let go.

I now want you to bring to mind an event, experience, or any past memory that filled you with joy and happiness. It doesn't matter how big or small, as long as it's a time when you were very happy. Take yourself to that moment and relive it now. Hear what you heard, see what you saw, feel how you felt. Take yourself there and feel that happiness. Experience it again. Feel it in your body now.

Now think of another memory, a time when you were very grateful. Take yourself to that memory and feel your entire body and energy shifting into that appreciative state. Relive that moment and allow that gratitude to fill your body and whole being.

Now, remember another time from the past. A time when you felt effortless and boundless love. Take yourself to that memory. See what you saw, hear what you heard, and feel what you felt in that moment. Allow this feeling of love to immerse your entire body and whole being. Live in that feeling now, and let it take over you.

As you leave that memory now, say mentally, "My heart is filled with peace. My heart is filled with joy. My heart is filled with love. My heart is filled with peace. My heart is filled with joy. My heart is filled with love. My heart is filled with peace. My heart is filled with joy. My heart is filled with love." As you now just breathe and be, your mind and body are calm and centered. Everything that has been is what needed to be. At this moment, you're connecting with that inner energy, inner power, and inner body. Feel the energy flowing through you. Feel it even stronger. See a glowing light flowing through you. This is healing light. See your body being healed by this glowing energy of light, allowing you to heal.

See all the things in this life that you want your body to be, how you want to feel, how you want to look. The change is being made as this energy flows through you. Begin to feel that healing, that shift in frequency. Experience the new sensations as healing is created now. Experience the healing throughout the body. All you need is within you now: all the energy, all the love, all the happiness, all the joy, all the peace, all the gratitude. As you imagine it and create it within the body, all you need is within you now. All the energy, all the love, all the happiness, all the joy, all the peace, all the gratitude.

As you connect with this awareness and create it within your body, you feel the healing. Mentally say to yourself, "My heart is filled with peace. My heart is filled with joy. My heart is filled with love." Create that healing and experience healing throughout your body. Mentally say, "All I need is within me now. All the energy, all the love, all the joy, all the gratitude is within me now. As I imagine it, I create it in my body." Allow that energy to shine through you. All the love, all the gratitude, all the joy. Trust it is done. Your destiny is yours. Feel the energy. It is already done. Enjoy the peace. Enjoy that love, joy, gratitude.

Within you is healing energy. Expand this energy and radiate it into the world. With his energy, you have the will to create the love, gratitude, happiness, and healing you've always wanted. Soak in this knowing for a few more minutes until you feel complete. Then, take deep breaths in and out and bring yourself back into the present moment in the room or environment you're in. Carry this feeling and your healing into everything else you do.

Namaste.

# Manifesting Joy and Happiness

For this meditation, find a comfortable position, seated or lying down comfortably on your back, and sink into that relaxed feeling. Make sure you're in a safe space without interruptions or distractions.

Do a quick full-body scan, noticing the areas where tension is present. From head to toe, give yourself permission to let go of tension and soften into this moment. Choose to relax into your body. Realize that making this choice to relax is just like making a choice to be happy. Happiness is a choice you can make, but it requires present moment awareness. Notice how becoming aware of your body enables you to know which areas are tense and which need some healing energy. As you bring your attention to this present moment, you activate your ability to choose to relax. You'll discover that being present also gives you the ability to choose to be happy...and it all starts with becoming more presently focused. Let's spend a few minutes now tuning into your body.

Now imagine you can just let the outside world fade away. Focusing on yourself, feel your breath coming in and out. Begin to notice anything you notice within you. Do you notice how you're already beginning to relax? Breathe in and breathe out slowly. Release any stress or tension. Allow your breath to calm you in all areas of your body. Feel yourself relaxing even more, and begin to notice your emotions coming and going. Emotions come and go once they are acknowledged. Allow yourself to have these emotions. Once you allow for them, they are able to flow and clear through, so allow them to just flow out of you.

Notice now that this practice is making you more present, more serene. Notice how your body is right now. Feel comfort kicking in. Now, start to think of a few things that bring you joy. Perhaps they are memories of when you were joyful. Notice where in your body this feeling of joy is more pronounced. Is it butterflies in your tummy or lightness in your heart? Now, add a gentle smile to your face. Allow these feelings of joy to amplify. More memories are coming to mind of when you were happy, joyful, laughing. Notice how you feel right now. How do you experience joy? Take note of how you feel right now, almost as if you're taking a picture of exactly how joy feels for you. Allow yourself to create a map of joy within yourself.

You have created the beautiful feeling of happiness just by thinking about it. Allow yourself to be happy now. Recall memories and people that make you happy. Perhaps you have a pet, a friend, a loved one who fills you with joy. Perhaps creating art or music brings joy to you. Feel this energy of joy pulsating through your body. You are allowed to be happy no matter what's going on around you. This is your birthright, your choice—to be happy. Soak in this meditative state and feel the power of joy running through your entire body.

Notice how beautiful you are. The beautiful joy you can now radiate to others warms you up. Bring a big smile to your face now. Let the joy show in your facial expression.

Now, imagine you're breathing in joyfully and deeply. Your oxygen is now mixed in with joy, and you're breathing it in and breathing it out. Fully and deeply take in the fresh oxygen that's filled with the beauty of happiness. Remember that you can carry this feeling of joy and happiness no matter where you go because now you have it within.

To finish your joyful affirmation, repeat the following joyful affirmations:

> *I am blessed. I am blessed. I am blessed.*
> *I am a happy person. I am a happy person. I*
> *am a happy person.*
> *Happiness finds me everywhere I go. Happi-*
> *ness finds me everywhere I go. Happiness*
> *finds me everywhere I go.*
> *No matter the circumstance, I can choose*
> *happiness. No matter the circumstance, I can*
> *choose happiness. No matter the circum-*
> *stance, I can choose happiness.*
> *Happiness is my choice. Happiness is my*
> *choice. Happiness is my choice.*

Notice how these affirmations are shifting your frequency. Spend another minute or so repairing these positive, happy affirmations and shifting your reality. And remember, no matter the situation, you can choose to bring joy from within.

So, the next time you're stuck in a difficult or trying situation, recall this wonderful state you've been able to create here in just a few minutes. Summon it and allow it to take over. Feel it in your body.

May you go into the world and bring happiness with you no matter what happens. Bring your awareness back into the room and environment you're in as you get out of this meditative state. Simply go about your day in this state of joy.

## Manifesting Love

If you've struggled to find or maintain healthy, loving relationships in your life, this meditation on love is for you. You might be single and looking for your soulmate or in a relationship you're hoping to transform. In both cases, the following script will show you how to manifest more love in your life.

Before we begin, I invite you to set aside all your preconceived notions of love and romantic relationships. Allow yourself the possibility of becoming aware of something new and be open to ideas that may feel counterintuitive at first. Why? Because if your current thinking was sufficient enough, you'd already have the love you seek. So, set aside your biases and suspend disbelief. Allow me to paint a new picture for you that will raise your frequency naturally and expand your current awareness. See your mind as a clean canvas upon which we can write a new love story. With your mind open and energetically aligned with this new story, you'll vibrate in harmony with the desire, and the universe will respond with evidence to match that internal reality.

Take a moment to get comfortable now. Find a relaxing spot where you won't be distracted or interrupted over the next several minutes. A good time to go through this script is in the morning before leaving the house for the day, but you can choose an ideal time and environment that suits your preference.

Take a moment now to go within and listen. Take deep breaths in and out and just listen within. Do this for about 30 seconds.

Check in with your body and pay attention to what it's telling you. Could your body become more comfortable? Is your current sitting or lying-down position giving you maximum relaxation? Could you relax a certain area a little more and release more tension? Notice whether your jaw is clenched or relaxed. What about your shoulders and forehead?

Do a light body scan and find any area that feels tight and tense, then let go of any unnecessary effort, clenching, or tightening. Become gentle and fluid like water. Allow softness and ease to wash over your entire body. Let your muscles release and find ease. Reach for that sense of stillness, fluidity, and ease. Do this for about 30 seconds.

Your mind is now becoming more open, and your body is more relaxed. The mind-body connection is taking root now because as the body relaxes, it signals the mind to relax as well. And as we become more and more relaxed, we put ourselves in the best state to manifest. Notice how relaxed yet focused you are in this present moment. Feel good about bringing yourself to this moment of ease, grounded-ness, and focused relaxation.

Start to notice your breathing again. Take a deep breath in and out, and notice the ease with which this happens without any effort on your end. There's nowhere else to be but right here and now. Nothing to do but just be here now. Your mind is becoming more centered with each breath. You easily let go of thoughts, things, demands, to-do lists, and the past. There is only this moment. Breath in...breathe out...take it one deep breath at a time, and just allow yourself to be. Your physical sensations are becoming heightened as you become more present. You are in tune with every physical sensation in your body, watching and listening closely. Notice the subtle flow of breath that occurs throughout your body. Your breath and body are becoming the only thing in your reality now. You are focused on the moment in a relaxed way. You're open to receiving new ideas and new experiences. You feel peaceful and harmonious. Practice this state of relaxed focus for one more minute.

We are now in the ideal state for manifesting a new reality of effortless, unconditional love. And the truth is, love is endless and effortless. You don't need to do anything to have love in your life—it's already here. You just need to allow it to flow through you. The barriers that have blocked love are the ones we need to dissolve so you can have love from the inside and outside. Barriers to endless, effortless love originate from fear. The fear of getting hurt, being rejected, or loneliness. But all these barriers are created by the mind. And if the mind can create them, it can also dissolve them. And that's what we're doing here and now, melting away these fears that have stood in the way of love in your life.

Start to notice something melting and being dissolved within you. See it melting and dissolving into the ocean of love. There is no fear powerful enough to withstand the love that is always within you. You are loved. Spend a moment now imagining all the barriers and resistance and negative biases that have lingered in your life around love melting into a peaceful ocean of love. Do this for one minute.

What does love feel like in your body? Is it deep peacefulness? A sense of relaxation? Safety and comfort? Joy? All those feelings? Allow yourself to feel and tune into all these feelings as they become accessible to you in this present moment. Experience the love that is starting to fill your entire body now. Feel the effortless love filling each cell in your body. You are filled with love from the tips of your toes to the crown of your head. Allow yourself to be filled from the inside with love like a vase being filled with water. Let this boundless love flow and fill you until it overflows out of the top of your head. You now sense it cascading down all around you. This boundless, effortless, infinite love is always yours.

Spend a few moments experiencing the feelings of love filling you and overflowing from the inner world into the outer world now. Do this for about one minute.

Notice how full of love you are. And as you are this being filled with love, is there anything missing, really? Do you need anything from another? There's nothing to need, but there's plenty you can enjoy and share. By filling yourself first with boundless effort-less love, you

vibrate and radiate this energy, and you begin to draw toward you others who are vibrating at this same level. Instead of seeking to draw the love out of another person, you are overflowing with infinite love from within, and others on the same frequency are magnetized to your loving light. Whether you desire to draw a new person in your life through this love or draw the most loving responses and actions out of your current partner, the way to do it is by going within first. Be all the love you could ever need, and the world outside matches you with people and experiences that correspond to that created state.

Now, I invite you to visualize walking through the world as a fountain of boundless, effortless love. Notice how bright and vibrant the world is from this new state. People are behaving with more compassion and kindness toward you because they can feel you need nothing from them. People are seeing you for who you really are. They understand and honor you. You are filled with satisfaction and joy. You are never lonely. You are always fulfilled. Every relationship in your life feels more positive and harmonious. You see the beauty in others and attract the most effortless love from them.

Bask in this vibrational knowing for a few moments. Allow these statements and images of infinite love into your life. Do this for two minutes.

Now that you've tuned into the essence of love that lies within you, it's time to shift perspective and reframe your worldview. Repeating positive affirmations in this relaxed state will enable you to reprogram your subconscious mind so you come into alignment with this new reality of love and maintain that vibrational knowing. You can repeat these phrases mentally or out loud; what matters is that you connect to the energy of the words. Allow these statements to flow through you, and influence your perspective and frequency. Repeat after me:

*All the love I could ever desire is already*

*within me. All the love I could ever desire is already within me. All the love I could ever desire is already within me.*

*I am one with love. I am made of love. I am love. I am one with love. I am made of love. I am love. I am one with love. I am made of love. I am love.*

*I easily and effortlessly attract loving experiences and people into my life. I easily and effortlessly attract loving experiences and people into my life. I easily and effortlessly attract loving experiences and people into my life.*

*The people in my life respond to me with love. The people in my life respond to me with love. The people in my life respond to me with love.*

*I see love in everything and everyone. I see love in everything and everyone. I see love in everything and everyone.*

Repeat your favorite set of affirmations several times now. Whichever words resonate most at this moment and cause you to feel loved and nurtured are the ones to repeat the most. Do this for about two more minutes.

Notice how you're feeling now. Observe the shift in perspective today as you go about interacting with others in your life. One day at a time, seeding this truth about love will bring you closer to the passion and fulfillment your heart has been seeking all this time.

Take a few more deep breaths, come out of this meditative state, and enjoy the rest of your day.

## Connecting with Your Soulmate Meditation

Practice this guided meditation in a comfortable position. Take a moment to adjust your sit bones so that they feel even on either side. If you're sitting in a chair, plant your feet firmly on the ground with your legs uncrossed. Adjust your spine so that you are sitting tall and confident. Now allow yourself to open up your heart by rolling your shoulders back. Allow your chest and you're heart's energy center to open up. Place your palms on your lap facing upwards, and if you feel comfortable, you may gently close your eyes.

Allow yourself to focus on your breath. Take a deep inhale, feel your stomach expand and release the breath, and feel your stomach contract. Throughout the course of this mediation, let your breath be intentional. Really allow yourself to fully breathe in on every inhale, offering nourishment to your body and soul, and fully releasing on every exhale. If possible, allow each inhale to equal the length of each exhale. This creates a beautiful rhythm and pattern. And as you breathe, allow yourself to focus on the energy center of your heart located in the middle of your chest and approximately two inches inward. As you focus on the present moment, allow yourself to be open, willing, and ready to accept your soul's highest love. That soul match that incarnated in this life with you—your soulmate.

Allow yourself to envision that you're seated on top of a hill. There are no trees around you. As far as your eyes can see, there's nothing but rolling hills full of soft, lush grass. And because there are no trees, you can see all the way out to the horizon. Looking out at the hills symbolizes the ups and downs you've been through in your life that have led you to where you are now. At this moment, you are ready and open to connecting with your soulmate.

Allow yourself to feel grateful for all the ups and downs you've been through that have led you to this moment. As you feel the readiness inside you, allow yourself to open up and connect with your soulmate. Recognize that they might not be ready; they might not be at the place that you are. Allow yourself to say to them: I love and accept you. I welcome you in whenever you're ready.

Allow yourself to take a long and deep inhale, and whenever you're ready, let the breath go with a sigh as you release your attachment to needing them to be here right now. True love and acceptance of your soulmate allow them to be on their own timeline just as you have been on yours. And this openness, this patience, this love for them wherever they are on their journey allows you to be a magnet attracting them in the perfect timeline. You allow yourself to be open without being controlling, and that enables you both to become an energetic match and for everything to work out in the highest, most loving way. And even though your soulmate isn't physically present with you, allow yourself to sense, feel, and bask in that infinite love you share. Relax in this boundless love and feel the energetic presence. Notice how this feels within you. Notice how this alters your energy and state of mind. Feel it uplifting your even more. What do you feel capable of in their presence? How do you carry yourself in their presence? How do you show up in life when you know they are with you? Trust and know that even when they are not physically with you, you can connect with their energy, feel their love, and offer them love. You have the ability to feel as you would if they were physically around you. Quite often, as soon as you let go of the need for them to be here with you physically, and you start loving them from wherever they are and in whatever they're doing, the timelines speed up, and you come into each other's lives. But first, it starts with loving and accepting yourself and them, no matter their timeline. Let your soulmate be free to be themself. It's time to stop trying to force or control them to be physically here with you now. Instead, simply enjoy the fact that you know they exist and you are connected. You know you're both going through whatever you need to go through so you may meet at the perfect time.

For the next few moments, send appreciation to them—wherever they are, whatever they're doing. Say in your heart, "I love and accept you. I appreciate you. I know we will meet when the timing is right."

Take this feeling of love, acceptance, and appreciation with you. As you bring your awareness back to your physical body, feel grateful you don't have to control anything because it's all destined to work out. Roll your shoulders now, wiggle your fingers and toes, and open your eyes. Take a deep inhale and exhale. Go out into the day in this knowing that your soulmate is with you even now.

## Manifesting Wealth and Money

This powerful meditation will help you become a magnet for money. For best results, I encourage you to go through this script with binaural beats in the background to aid you in tapping into a higher frequency faster.

Find a quiet place where you won't be interrupted or distracted for 15-20 minutes. Sit comfortably, seated or lying down with your back straight and your palms facing up in receiving mode. Take a deep breath in, and slowly exhale. Allow your mind to settle and release the thoughts that come. This is your time...surrender to this moment. I want you to take any fear, hesitation, lack, or feelings of desperation towards money and let them all go. It's time to wipe the slate clean. You now know that you don't need anything from the outside. You already have everything you need, and abundance is always available to you. Money is energy; it's currency, and you are going to tap into that currency now.

I want you to take a few moments and allow yourself to visualize and feel exactly how it would feel if you already had all the money you needed, just as though it was an unlimited resource now available to you. How would your life look? How would you feel? Spend a few moments visualizing and feeling what it would be like to have more money than you could ever possibly need.

Breathe in this feeling for a few more minutes.

Now I want you to visualize a glowing light flowing through your body. This warm, glowing energy is flowing from the top of your head all the way down to your toes. This glowing, flowing light is the energy of money, and that's all that money is. It's simply energy that you can attract, and it's now flowing directly from the universe through your body and into your current reality.

Allow the energy to flow through you and feel it becoming part of your physical reality. Don't force it;

simply allow it to flow naturally and effortlessly. Soak in this flow for a few minutes.

Now, repeat the following affirmations and allow them to sink deep into your subconscious mind. Focus on feeling the energy of the words as you memorize them.

> *I am a money magnet. I am a money magnet.*
> *I am a money magnet.*
> *I am grateful. I am grateful. I am grateful.*
> *I trust in the universe to deliver exactly what*
> *I want. The universe always provides.*
> *Money is constantly pouring in. I have*
> *unlimited abundance. I have everything I*
> *could ever want or need. Money is continu-*
> *ously pouring in. I have unlimited abun-*
> *dance. I have everything I could ever want or*
> *need. Money is constantly pouring in. I have*
> *unlimited abundance. I have everything I*
> *could ever want or need.*

Allow yourself to have a few moments of feeling deep, profound gratitude for this new awareness and new frequency.

Now, take your left palm and place it over your heart, then take your right palm and place it over your heart. Take a deep inhale, then a slow exhale to the count of four. Feel the love, abundance, joy, peace, and knowing that the universe is providing. Allow your emotions to be soaked in the knowing that wealth is here, and as you do, you allow money to immediately start coming your way. You are a powerful vessel, and money can come to you instantly without you trying hard. It will arrive at the most unexpected times in the most unexpected scenarios with your effort. These are the ways of the universe, and these are the powers that lie within you.

Slowly breathe yourself back into your current environment. Slowly find your senses again as you continue to breathe in and out. Carry this knowing with you as you go into the day and engage in your usual activities.

## Manifest Your Dreams

Abundance is creative energy. The creative energy flows to you and through you. It has no form—you give it form. Anything you can imagine in your mind, you can manifest in your reality. There are no limitations aside from those you place on yourself.

In this guided meditation script, we want to open you up to connect with this creative flow so you can cultivate a divine vision and attract it toward yourself.

Begin by placing your body in a supported and relaxed position. Make sure your body is comfortable whether you're sitting or lying down. Start taking deep breaths in and out, and let yourself relax. Breathe in deeply, filling your lungs with air, then exhale all stress and tension. As you exhale, imagine breathing out all the anxiety you've been holding. Do this breathing exercise two more times.

Allow your mind to wander around what might be 1-5 years down the line for you if you truly become the powerful creator of your reality. Let your breath become deeper, your body even more relaxed, and just surrender to this moment. Allow your consciousness to become detached from your surroundings. Let yourself float into your divine vision and see what the next level of your life looks like. How do you feel as you go about your day? What does the world look like? What goals have you accomplished?

Observe and expand your vision so you can be filled with this new light. This is your dream life.

Bask and soak in this vision for several minutes. Once you feel completely immersed in the reality of this new state, bring your awareness to your heart center and feel grateful.

Notice the gentle rise and fall of your chest as you continue to breathe in and out. Each breath takes you ever deeper into a feeling of gratitude and peace.

You now become aware of a beautiful golden light surrounding you. This sparkling golden light is the creative energy of the universe. It's powerful and divine. You allow this golden light to enter into your being through the crown of your head. Feel it as it runs through your body, giving you a warm, glowing sensation. It fills your head, scalp, forehead, jaw, and mouth. It moves into your neck, upper back, and shoulders, then down your arms, elbows, and hands right to the tips of your fingers. This beautiful light glows as it moves down your spine into your lower back, pelvis, and sitting bones. It shines warmly as it moves into your throat, chest, heart, and stomach. It moves down your legs, and now into your knees and feet right down to the tips of your toes, filling your whole body with this powerful, creative energy.

Every cell in your body is now filled with this limitless golden light. And it shines brightly, eradicating any beliefs you've been holding onto that you're not good enough. That you can't have your dream manifest. That there isn't enough. That it's not possible... and any other beliefs that have been holding you back. This glowing, golden light surrounds all these limiting beliefs and dissolves them once and for all. Gone.

Now you are free to be all that you can be.

As this powerful golden light fills you completely, you radiate abundance, and you realize the creative power you are. And you smile gratefully for this realization. You now use your imagination to create the life of your dreams...beautiful, bright, and abundant. Whatever you envision in your future, you will create. You live in a place that makes you deeply happy. You live in a home you love filled with everything you treasure. It is precisely what you wanted. You have positive, real relationships with people you love and who nourish you. You have a romantic relationship that feels magical. A partner who absolutely adores you and whom you adore entirely. Someone with whom you can share your life of abundance, laughter, and joy.

You have amazing friendships with fabulous, fun, and interesting people who make you laugh, and encourage and inspire you. You have a gorgeous family with whom you share special moments. Loving and accepting each other just as you are and celebrating the precious time you have together. You work, love going to work, and have found meaning in what you do. It makes your heart come alive and feel inspired daily. You live a life of great prosperity. You never worry about money. You have more than you ever thought possible. Everything you want is yours, and you're very generous with your money. You have the time and freedom to do everything you've always wanted to do. Now you can spend your time doing more of the things you love. You can travel, pick up new hobbies, and so much more. It feels good to wake up each morning with this sense of freedom. You have a vibrantly healthy body you take good care of. You feed it nourishing foods and beverages, and your body responds with optimal health and abundant energy. You have the time and ability to give back to the world. You have it all, and you feel inspired to make a difference in the world. You serve others and the good of all. You love doing this, and it brings you immeasurable joy. You have the life of your dreams now.

As you send this reality out into the universe, this beautiful golden light within you glows brightly...so brightly, now expanding out from you in all directions. Ever more brightly, reaching out and filling every inch of the universe with its powerful creative force...and it is done.

You have the life of your dreams, and you can live in positive expectations now. Go forward into your day, seeing abundance in everything and everyone. See through the eyes of the powerful creator you are. Smile and share your joy, excitement, and love with the world. Walk in the knowledge of your divine vision with which you are aligned in this moment. You are amazing.

When you're ready, bring your awareness back into the room. Start taking five deep breaths and slowly become more aware of your body and present environment. Take another deep breath, become aware of the presence in the room, feel yourself in your body, and become fully present and aware of your surroundings.

Thank you for going through this meditation. All is well, and your dream life is here.

Namaste.

# Manifest Success

In this meditation, our intention is to raise your frequency and enable you to discover the keys to experiencing success in all areas of life. Success is very subjective and can at times feel elusive, especially when one is not clear on what success looks like.

So what does success mean to you? What would a successful life look like? Bring these questions to mind as we enter into this meditative state. Your definition might change from year to year, and that's okay. Success should evolve as you evolve. What you considered success as a teenager cannot be what you view as success today. Your definition of success will probably be different from mine, and that's okay, too. We must all consciously and intentionally seek to identify and define our desires and images of success in our lives. That's what this meditation is designed to help you discover. It will help you align with your vision of success so the law of attraction can start matching you up with supporting evidence.

Make sure you're seated comfortably for this meditation. You don't need to worry about keeping your eyes open because you can still receive the energy and perspective shift that this and all meditation scripts offered in this book provide. What matters is that you make yourself comfortable in an environment with zero distractions and interruptions.

Begin to relax your body. Imagine letting go of your immediate environment and current circumstances. Let go of your day, let go of the world, and let go of the thoughts, conversations, and opinions of other people. To identify your heart's desire and, in turn, your vision of success, you have to tune into your heart and release everything else.

Begin by feeling your body and just notice how you're doing today. Feel all the sensations in your body, even if some are a bit unpleasant. Notice the tension or discomfort wherever that might be, but do so without judgment. Simply observe.

Bring your awareness to your breath and notice how effortlessly it flows in and out through your body. See if you can gel with the rhythm of your breathing. With each inhale, you become more present, and as you exhale, you release any and all tension. A feeling of deep peace begins to wash over your body as you continue this practice. Don't overthink it or force it; simply go with the flow of your natural rhythm and sink into this peaceful feeling for a few moments. Do this practice for one minute.

Welcome to your first experience with success. By successfully tuning into your body in this present moment and finding peace, you have met with success. Success is what you make of it, and you are capable of achieving more success every single day. It starts with present-moment awareness. The more present you are, the easier it will be to notice the small and big accomplishments in each moment. The more you notice your success and celebrate it with deep gratitude, the more you align with that frequency, and the law of attraction continues to serve you more things to feel good about.

To shift your mindset to look for and receive more success, it's helpful to first notice how you might be setting yourself up for failure rather than success.

Take a moment now to think about yourself and the common experience of daily living. Imagine you've built a box around you that limits your perspective. This box is made up of all the rules you have for yourself about what it means to be successful. Perhaps you've conditioned your brain to believe that success is hard or that you need to be more perfect, healthy, wealthy, or educated to be successful. These limiting ideas have become thick walls that keep you stuck in experiences of failure. These beliefs become the reason you never meet success. All you have to do is shift your mindset, and you'll discover that you have been successful all along.

Now, spend a few moments identifying which limiting beliefs have kept you stuck in a tiny box of limitations. What impossible standards are you holding yourself to? What ideas of failure do you seem to keep repeating over and over again? What ideas of success seem unattainable to you? Observe the answers that come without judgment. Allow yourself to become aware of what's really going on in your mind. Observe your limiting box for a minute with great compassion.

Now, imagine you're going to destroy this box that has kept you stuck in limitations. Visualize the walls dissolving away as ice melts under the warm sun. See these limiting thoughts melt away into nothingness. Your old ideas of failure and success no longer exist. You are free to create a new story with a new perspective. Imagine yourself floating in a feeling of spaciousness. There's so much room for you to create and try new things. Your success is easy to achieve, and there's no end to how much success you can create in your life. Celebrate this new understanding and feel grateful your mind has come to this awareness.

I now want you to think back to when you achieved something you were really proud of. Recall that memory of great success and explore the feelings you had. What did you feel? Can you feel it now in your body? Bring these feelings back to life here and now as you allow your frequency to rise and match up with the energy field of that successful version of you. Take about two minutes to do this.

Notice how you're feeling in your body. What emotions are you experiencing? Is it joy? Creativity? Pride? Strength? Love? All of the above? Can you identify what success feels like to you? Breathe into these wonderful feelings. It's wonderful and easy to relive moments of success in your past. And what's equally powerful is to revisit moments of perceived failure and rewrite the story about those experiences.

So, let's do that now. Travel back in time and recall an experience of failure. Was it really all bad, or can you identify some nuggets of wisdom and success? So often, we focus intently on what's not working or not going well that we forget to celebrate the small wins that did occur or the transformational lessons that set us on a new and better path. Perhaps the hidden success is that you showed up, got out of your comfort zone, and tried something new and risky—even that is worth celebrating.

Spend a few moments rewriting the stories around your past failure. Notice how the perceived failures helped you grow and become a better person. Acknowledge the success that was hidden in the failures all along. Do this for about 3 minutes.

Now that you've stepped into the mindset of a highly successful person, it's time to discover what success truly means to you in your heart. Visualize that you're floating in freedom. There's nothing else in this moment. There's no society to measure up to. There's no one to analyze or judge your desires. It's just you and your ideas, dreams, and beliefs. Imagine diving deeper into your heart center and unlocking the yearnings and secrets that have been locked up for years. Maybe since childhood. What does success really mean to you in your heart? Is it sharing your creativity? Is it becoming a better person every day or making someone else's life easier? There's no right or wrong answer. If you could wave a magic wand and replace your world with the vision of success your heart longs for, what would that look like? What would it feel like? Spend a few minutes listening to and seeing the answer in your mind's eye. Do this for about three minutes.

Now that you have a clear picture of what success looks like for you, achieving it becomes the next logical step. Achieving it will also feel effortless because this is something you want, and the mind and heart cannot want something they aren't capable of creating. So, relax and take a deep breath because your success is guaranteed. You are already on the path of success because you've discovered what success means to you.

Now it's time to use positive statements of affirmations and take consistent actions toward those goals. Repeat these statements with deep feeling:

*Success is my birthright. I am successful. Success follows me everywhere I go. Success is my birthright. I am successful. Success follows me everywhere I go. Success is my birthright. I am successful. Success follows me everywhere I go.*

*I am a successful person. I know how to create my own success. I am a successful person. I know how to create my own success. I am a successful person. I know how to create my own success.*

*I welcome more success into my life. I welcome more success into my life. I welcome more success into my life.*

*I show up as a success, and the world reflects that back to me. I celebrate my successes daily, both big and small. I show up as a success, and the world reflects that back to me. I celebrate my successes daily, both big and small. I show up as a success, and the world reflects that back to me. I celebrate my successes daily, both big and small.*

Spend another minute or two soaking in these positive statements. Allow these positive phrases to shift your inner and outer reality, to raise your frequency.

Feel your energy field shifting and aligning with the highest version of yourself.

Take a deep breath now and acknowledge the work you've done. Trust that a transformation has occurred. Remind yourself that you have the ability to create success each day, starting today.

Bring your awareness back into your present environment as you continue to breathe slowly. Wiggle your toes and fingers, come out of the meditation, and go back into the world with his new mindset and perspective.

Namaste.

# Bonus: Law of Attraction Affirmations for Success, Prosperity, and Manifesting your Dream Life

I am transmitting frequencies. I am choosing the frequencies I transmit. I know that whatever frequency I send out returns to me multiplied. I choose to emit a frequency of love, success, health, prosperity, peace, and joy. I deserve a great life. I am worthy of having all I want. I am a powerful creator. I am limitless. I am creating the life I love now. I am seeing myself as positive, joyful, and peaceful now. I am radiating love—love for myself and love for others. I am balanced, centered, and calm. I am living a peaceful, empowered life. I am living in the knowledge that I am safe, and all is well. I am living from a place of mindfulness, harmony, and contentment. I am flourishing. I feel a deep sense of well-being within myself, and I go about my days with joy in my heart. I am aware of how precious life is. I am aware of how precious life is, and I celebrate the gift of life every day, in every way. Every fiber of my being radiates positive energy. I am aware of how blessed I am. I am grateful. Thank you. Thank you for my life of well-being, positivity, and joy.

# Conclusion

Although we've come to the end of our quest in this book, the journey has only begun for you. Everything and anything you could ever want to be, do, have, and experience is yours, but you need to understand the laws that govern our lives as human beings. We are far grander than these physical bodies, and the real game isn't played at this physical level. Instead, it's all happening in the mind, governed by laws that are as immutable as the laws of physical science. To achieve what you most desire in life, you must align yourself with said laws.

Now that you've learned the truth about the law of attraction, the law of vibration, and all the other spiritual laws of success, it's time to sit in the driver's seat and take ownership of your life. In this book, you've learned what manifestation really is, how the law of attraction works, and why most struggle to manifest their desires. You've discovered that there's more to attracting and manifesting desires than sheer willpower or relentless action. Yes, taking action is a critical part of the process, but it cannot be a substitute for vibrational alignment. You've also learned about the two driving forces and how they impact what you manifest. When we are rooted in fear, the emotions that rule our minds make it impossible to manifest joyfully or naturally sustain success. And since most of the world is fear-focused, it is an individual responsibility to shift from a consciousness of fear to love because only then do we become joyful manifestors. Attracting from a state of love will never fail or disappoint because love casts out all fear and doubt.

With all this reading under your belt, what's next? Most people would put down this book and still struggle to implement what they've learned. To ensure that doesn't happen to you, here are your next practical steps. Consider each step the implementation of all the theoretical concepts we've covered in this book, and if there are chapters that stood out for you, go back and reread them a few times until they sink deeply into your subconscious.

**Step One**: Get to know yourself and the limiting beliefs that have held you back.

Before identifying your burning desire, you must dedicate time to learn more about yourself. The more self-awareness you have, the easier it will be to recognize blind spots, triggers, etc. Self-awareness is also the best way to ensure that the desire you pick will be true to you and not just an inherited paradigm. So, invest more time in educating yourself about your mind and how it works, the spiritual laws of success, and what it means to be a spiritual being having a human experience. You are more than your body, thoughts, and emotions. Behind those entities, there is an ever-present "observer," and you want to reconnect that awareness.

Let this book be one of the many aids that bring you in closer contact with that silent observer. Spend time in quiet reflection. Ask deep questions, even if you don't have answers. Questions such as "Who am I really?" and "What would I love to become in this lifetime?" are deep and often scary questions, but extremely necessary. The more you train yourself to access those more profound aspects of your being, the more fulfilling your personal development will be.

**Step Two.** Identify and replace limiting beliefs.

The late Dr. Wayne Dyer said, "If you change the way you look at things, the things you look at change." To me, that's a perfect prescription for taking control of things I cannot control. If I am currently experiencing financial lack or cannot find employment, I must put all my effort into changing the perspective, thoughts, and emotions I have around this topic. And as I control and shift, the things beyond my control (e.g., where my next job will come from) must change. How? The next job interview or the next client to whom I try to sell will meet me in a different emotional and psychological state. And that will make all the difference.

Now it's your turn to implement this concept into your life. What limiting beliefs have kept you stuck? How often do you say or think, "It's too late" or "I'll never be rich"? These are your limiting beliefs rearing their ugly heads. They are the breeding ground for self-doubt.

It's time to feed your subconscious mind new beliefs. Use meditations and affirmations to retrain your mind to think differently and place yourself on a "mental diet" so you can plant new thought seeds that replace old, outdated, and limiting beliefs about yourself.

**Step Three.** Have a clear, definite burning desire that is worthy of you.

My mentor Bob Proctor often says that when you're picking a desire or a goal, don't go for something that is worthwhile. Instead, go for something that feels worthy of you.

Why does he insist on this distinction? I think it's because no matter how big your desire might seem to you, nothing comes close to your magnificence. Even if your dream life involves owning a private jet and three homes in various exotic countries, none of that compares to who you are as a human being. If this idea feels like an exaggeration, you have a lot of work to do! Stay on this quest until you find out who you really are.

But I digress. This step is about identifying your heart's burning desire. What exactly does that dream life look like? Be as specific as you can, then follow the steps discussed in chapter six and work toward the realization of your desire.

**Step Four.** With your clearly defined desire and a workable plan to move you in the direction of your dreams, it's time to shift focus and send the right signals to the universe.

This step is where you do your part in raising your vibration, maintaining it, and connecting with the energy of what you desire to manifest. Then, you trust in the unfailing ability of the law of attraction.

**Step Five.** Take inspired action. Listen to the insights and intuitive nuggets that you get. Maintain a keen interest in all your activities and keep yourself in a state of positive expectation. Let your values enable you to be the best you can be in this present moment, expecting that your desired reality will match up in the right moment. That is where mindfulness practices and gratitude become powerful secret weapons because they keep you in that high frequency where all good things happen.

**Step Six.** Persist in holding yourself in that aligned state, knowing that your desire is here. It already exists as a spiritual prototype, and it's moving toward you as long as you keep moving toward it. And when you fall out of alignment, don't sit in despair too long.

Relinquish the need to judge and criticize yourself. The universe doesn't judge you; it simply responds to your vibration. As soon as you land on negativity, acknowledge it and quickly start building bridges to rise back into your highest vibrational frequency. And it doesn't matter how many times you fall. Be relentless and persistent in your commitment to your dreams. Always be connecting to a higher emotion no matter what's going on around you.

**Step Seven.** Integrate techniques and practices that will enable you to stay on the path of prosperity. It won't always be easy, but you know that now. So as long as you're prepared and have the toolkit I shared throughout this book, you'll have everything you need to survive even the worst storms. When the small wins come, appreciate and praise them because they are crumbs on the way to what you desire most. Even the tiniest success or sign of abundance is just as valuable as that ultimate desire. Remember, the universe doesn't know the difference between a dollar and a million dollars, so train your energy to be the same, and you will always win.

And there's so much more I could say, but this book would never end because in truth, understanding the game of life is a never-ending process. However, the one determining factor that remains fundamental to your success is you. So, choose to believe in yourself. Be graceful and patient with yourself as you grow. Believe you are powered by a divine force, the same stuff that powers the entire universe. And if that divine stuff has created such a marvelous and grand universe, surely you have everything you need within you to manifest this tiny dream life that your heart desires.

I say absolutely yes. You just needed to get to this point to realize it for yourself.

May your dream life be even more marvelous than you could have imagined.

Happy manifesting.

# SPECIAL BONUS!

> **GET 333 AFFIRMATIONS SENT DIRECTLY TO YOU + ACCESS TO ALL OF OUR FUTURE PUBLISHED BOOKS!**

**SIGN UP BELOW TO CLAIM YOUR BONUS!**

*SCAN W/ YOUR CAMERA TO JOIN!*

# Resources

Dyer, W. W. (2015, November 5). *Manifesting Your Desires*. Dr. Wayne W. Dyer. Retrieved January 28, 2022, from https://www.drwaynedyer.com/blog/manifesting-your-desires/

Deepak Chopra™. (2020, July 17). *Law of Attraction*. Retrieved January 28, 2022, from https://www.deepakchopra.com/articles/law-of-attraction/

Gallagher, S. (2018, January 16). *How the Law of Attraction Works*. Proctor Gallagher Institute. Retrieved January 28, 2022, from https://www.proctorgallagherinstitute.com/6809/how-the-law-of-attraction-works

Canfield, J. (2021, November 10). *A Complete Guide to Using the Law of Attraction*. Jack Canfield. Retrieved January 28, 2022, from https://www.jack-canfield.com/blog/using-the-law-of-attraction/

Hill, N., & Horowitz, M. (2019). *Think and Grow Rich* (*Original Classic Edition*) (Original ed.). G&D Media.

Printed in Great Britain
by Amazon

86550257R00169